What people are saying:

"...extremely helpful...informative ... *inspiring...feel much better about my finances."* (James Galvin, New York, NY)

"...very impressed with the quality of the information and your presentation!" (Rosemary Hume, Kansas City, MO)

"I have already begun to make money in the stock market. Your advice was simple and honest...it's as easy as you described." (Michelle de Jesus, San Francisco, CA)

"Excellent! Very informative!" (M. Gregg, Washington, DC)

"Excellent...interesting & funny...great information." (Linda Neilson, Bronx, NY)

"Very informative and enjoyable...even though I was stock market illiterate, this (book) is a real confidence booster." (Dinnis Lee, Victorville, CA)

"A wealth of information...a must read for the small investor." (Phyllis Durr, Washington, DC)

"Magnificent! For the first time in many years I feel like I understand the stock market and the right way to go about investing." (Tom Kay, Houston, TX)

"...both the class & the book are one of the best investments I have made..." (Bruce A. Hop, Austin, TX)

"fascinating and edifying...extremely helpful...clear, concise, well-reasoned...no gobbledygook..." (Marion the Librarian, Culver City, CA)

"Our most popular class..." (Communiversity, University of Missouri, Kansas City)

"...recommending it to everyone I know..." (Doris Gagnon, Overland Park, KS)

**Building Your Financial Portfolio
On $25 A Month (Or Less)**
© 2005

Bobbie Christensen
Eric Christensen

Effective Living Publishing
P. O. Box 232233
Sacramento, CA 95823
ELPBooks@aol.com
www.BooksAmerica.com

Published by Effective Living Publishing
P.O.Box 232233, Sacramento, CA 95823
(916) 422-8435 – orders (800) 929-7889
Email: ELPBooks@aol.com
Website: www.BooksAmerica.com

ISBN: 0-9729173-2-2

Books by Bobbie and Eric Christensen
Building Your Financial Portfolio On $25 A Month (Or Less), 4th edition ($15.95)
Adding To Your Financial Portfolio ($14.95)
Top 50 Best Stock Investments, 2nd edition ($19.95)
Building Your Debt-Free Life ($14.95)

Books by Bobbie Christensen
The Banker Chronicles (a mystery) ($14.95)
Building Your Dream Life: Career, Sex & Leisure ($14.95)
Getting A Free Education: The Key To Your Dream Job ($11.95)
Writing, Publishing & Marketing Your 1st Book (Or 7th) on a shoe-string budget ($15.00)

Add $4.00 for shipping and handling per shipment

Newsletter
Common Sense Portfolio, monthly ($25 for 1 year, $47 for 2 years)

To order, call 1-800-929-7889 (Mastercard & Visa accepted)
Or mail check or money order to:
BooksAmerica, PO Box 232233, Sacramento, CA 95823
Or visit:
www.BooksAmerica.com/ELPBooks

TABLE OF CONTENTS

1. What Stock Brokers Never Tell You

Welcome to the world of investing! We say welcome because this book is meant for the beginning investor as well as the investor who wants to find a safe, secure place to put their money, where it will grow 100% or more a year, but without having to spend a lot of time doing the research or worrying about their investments. If you lost a lot of money in your retirement account during the recession, you will learn how to take what is left and make it grow SAFELY this time so you will not have to worry about the next recession. You will also learn very important information on how to cut out stock broker fees and expenses thus keeping that money in your own pocket. We feel it is important for everyone to take charge of their own lives and their own finances rather than put $1,000 or $5,000 or all of your retirement money into an over-diversified mutual fund, pension plan, 401K, or IRA that has historically grown no more than 29% a year (based on the best performing mutual fund in 1999, the last good year of the 1990's boom economy) and at considerable risk.

You will learn through carefully outlined and step-by-step details how to find these safe companies as well as how to actually do the investing. We feel everyone in this country should have access to this important information without having to pay hundreds of dollars for books, tapes, or seminars. After all, free enterprise is what our country is based on and we should all take advantage of this right to invest that other countries do not enjoy. And the great thing about the stock market is that it is open to everyone regardless of age, sex, religion or ethnicity.

We are not brokers or financial managers and have no vested interest in any company mentioned in this book other than our own personal investments and/or personal research. Our purpose is strictly to educate and give you the tools that you never learned in school and that no stock broker will ever tell you about. We are retired bankers who have successfully used this method of investing for ourselves and thousands of others nationwide over the last 20 plus years.

After all, we all know we need to save, both for our own well-being and for the well-being of our country's economy. We have recently seen how certain other countries would like to destroy our economy. But September 11th has proven, once again, that our system of government works and our economy continues as strong as ever no matter what happens. In

2

the bombing of the World Trade Center, several of the largest brokerage firms in the country had their main offices destroyed to say nothing of losing some of their top executives. Yet, they continued to do business from their homes. Our system is as strong as our people are.

Too often we are lead to believe that we need to be rich (or at least have $1,000) in order to invest our money. No you don't! To make this information available to everyone, this book is specifically written to be easily understood by anyone from 13 years old to 90. After you have started your investment plan, share this with your children and grandchildren or, if you are a teacher, with your students. The more our citizens know about how our economy operates and how the stock market functions, the safer and stronger we all become.

The point of this book is to show you how to use just $25 (or less) a month to build your portfolio. So first, let's look at an example of what we will be talking about.

Let's say that in 1994 you bought $100 worth of shares in Johnson & Johnson and left it there for 10 years. During that time you did not put any more money into it, but there were dividends and stock splits (we will talk about them later). At the end of the 10 years, in 2004, that $100 investment would now be worth over $445.88. This includes stock splits, dividend reinvestment, and market appreciation during those 10 years. Keep in mind that we are talking about long-term investing because you cannot have safety without looking at the long-term period. And long-term to us means investing for a minimum of 5 years (we will explain why later), but we much prefer 10 years for safety. If you average out the growth in this over the 10 years, you will find that you had an average annual growth of 346%. But this is not what we are talking about. We are talking about building your financial portfolio on $25 a month. Therefore, if you bought that $100 worth of stock and then added another $25 every month for the 10 year period, your stock would now be worth over $14,000. This is what we mean by safe, secure investing.

However, if your budget does not quite stretch to $25 a month, be aware that there are other companies that require as little as a $10 monthly investment. Or did you just read our example and wonder what would happen if you put in $100 each month instead of only $25? What you are thinking is exactly right. The more money you put in, the bigger and faster it will grow. Shortly, we will talk about how much you should invest monthly.

Keep in mind that this book is for people who want to invest SAFELY but with tremendous GROWTH. Because you will be using a safe method, fluctuations in the stock market will not effect your investment, as we will demonstrate and you will be able to sleep nights without worrying.

This book is also for the person who does not find numbers or the stock market all that interesting and, thus, does not want to spend a lot of time on research. You must spend time every single day doing research if you want to invest in high-risk stock because you have to be constantly watching the market and making buying and selling decisions. With low-risk long-term investments, you make your decision choosing only from very safe businesses and do not have to look at it again until you need to retrieve some money. If you find this book very interesting and would like to learn more about investing, see the end of this book for information on its sequel, *Adding To Your Financial Portfolio*.

This is the 4th edition of this book since it was originally published in 1997. Many thousands of people have read previous editions and/or have attended one of our nationwide seminars. They are the ones who prove that this method of investing actually works. They are the ones who did not lose their retirement money during the recession.

2. Who Should Invest

Every citizen should be investing for their future. That means anyone from 10 years old to 65 or even older. You have all heard this a thousand times. Even if our parents did not tell you, you would have heard it on a newscast or some talk show. Everyone knows how important it is to save for the future, but how many of you are actually doing something about it? How many are just procrastinating and then one day, or more specifically on your 60th birthday, realize you have put it off for too long.

And what is the major reason for putting off saving, besides procrastination? It is the same reason we put off most things in life - - money. We tell ourselves that we just do not have anything extra to invest right now, but we will some day. Some day has come!

A few schools around the country have started trying to teach children about investing for the future. Some (unfortunately not many) students in this country, from high school through college, have had fun playing investment games where they pretend to pick and buy stocks and then watch what happens. In the standard classroom setting, students are given $100,000 (just pretend money) to invest in the stock market. This is an excellent educational tool to help teach our children about one aspect of our economy. But wouldn't it be even more fun to use real money to teach your children how to invest safely? Obviously, we are not going to give them $100,000, nor should we. The problem with the method being used in our schools is that it teaches our children that the only way you can invest in the market is if you already have a great deal of money sitting around. Just recently on our local news, a school using this program was highlighted. The interesting thing about this news segment was that, after taking this program, most of the students said that when they were out of school and had a high paying job, they would then invest in the stock market. Only two students understood that they could invest without having a huge amount of money. By giving anyone this much money in order to learn about the market, you are telling them that they **must** have this much money in order to be able to invest. This is just simply not true. However, if your intention is to discourage them from ever investing in their own future, you will do an excellent job of it. One reason this happens is that the teachers themselves do not understand how the stock market operates either.

What we should be teaching students, teachers, and everyone else in this country, is that the stock market is an opportunity we are all given no matter how much, or little, money you have. As parents, we usually encourage our teenagers to get a part-time job in order to learn about the work place and, hopefully, save some money to get their lives started or to go to college with. But, if that teenager is putting his or her money into a bank savings account, they quickly become discouraged at how little their money grows. Instead, they should follow the directions given here, invest $25 to $100 in a good safe stock, and watch their money grow much larger every year. And, if they do **not** follow these directions for **safely** investing their money but decide instead to choose risky investments, they will learn quickly why that is not a good idea and yet only risk losing $100 or less in the learning process.

We think nothing of putting checks we are given at our babies birth into a savings account for them. After all, we want to save for our baby's future. But why not put it into an investment that will be safe and yet will have a great deal more growth potential. In our previous example, we were talking about doing it for just 10 years. Think of the result if instead of opening that savings account, you bought or gave just one share of stock to that child who has another 17 or 18 years to save for their college education or to start their own business. Keep in mind that as soon as a child has a social security number (Federal law requires this by the April 15th following their birth date), they can have investments in their own name with the name of an adult with them. However, if this is for college expenses, make sure you take your name off the account as soon as the child is of legal age so that, when they sell the stock, taxes will be paid in the child's name rather than the adult's name. That is, a student is usually in a much lower tax bracket than the parent is.

Although we have been talking about children and young adults, it is safe to say that most people do not understand how the stock market works and, therefore, have developed the opinion that only the very rich segment of our population can earn "free" money in the stock market as well as other investment areas. You hear of someone buying $100,000 worth of stock and having it become $1,000,000 seemingly overnight and wish you could do the same thing. But, the majority of our population does not have $100,000 to invest. The majority do not even have the $1,000 to $5,000 minimum necessary to invest in a mutual fund and certainly not when they are in their twenties and just starting out in life. Yet that is the age that they should be saving for their first home or for retirement. The government starts taking social security out of your pay check immediately, so why shouldn't you take something out for your own financial future?

Of course, a regular savings account is an investment and you can put in just pennies if you want to, but it can be terribly boring watching your $10 grow by $.02 a month. With our investment plan you can watch it grow up to 100% a year or even much more, plus have the excitement of seeing a 3 for 1 split triple your investment "overnight". With our method you will be doing a little bit more work than putting money into a savings acount but earning a lot more.

We refer to this as "our" method of investing. However, we cannot take credit for this. If you read *The Wall Street Journal* every day for 5 years, you would already know about this method of investing. However, only a very small number of people read that paper at all, let alone on a daily basis. You will also see, as we go along, why no stock broker will ever tell you about this method of investing.

Some people have said that investing in the stock market, whether on your own or through an investment club or by way of mutual funds, is a legalized form of betting. Or perhaps you had parents like mine that taught you that everything in life is a gamble. You are gambling when you start a new job, get married, buy a house, and at many other times in your life. But we do not think of it as gambling because we feel we are investing in our future and using a very safe method to do so. When we marry, we know there is the possibility (and a very great possibility today) that it will not work out. Yet most of us will take that risk. Certainly one of the biggest risks we can take with our financial security is starting our own business, but thousands of people are doing just that every year, now more than ever. Most people, even kids, find a certain pride in having their lemonade stand, selling their extra produce, having a part-time consulting business, opening a computer training center, or any of the thousands of other choices in life. Having a small part-time business usually does not pose any threat to your financial well-being. But renting space, leasing equipment, hiring help, and opening a computer training center could be a threat.

Any of these life occurances can be done safely and without gambling if done correctly. Why do so many marriages fail? Because they did not get past the euphoria of love to what could happen in the future. Why do the majority of new small businesses fail within the first five years? Because they did not get past the sense of euphoria about being their own boss and find out how to do it correctly. However, you don't have to start your own business. Remember that when you invest in the stock market, you are investing in a company and becoming a part owner of it. Because of this, you need to do the same things you would do in starting your own business. That is, you need to research and find out if they know how to market themselves, if they have financial backing, if they have a proven history. In this book, we are going to explain how to do this research using just a few minutes of your time and, who knows, maybe you will learn things that will help you start your own successful business.

There is always the possibility of losing money when you invest it. However, by following our method, you will create minimum risk for your money with maximum gain! Again, this has been proven during the recent economic recession as well as over the past 100 years of market history.

3. Why Should You Invest

Learning about the financial world and enjoying the excitement of this legal form of gambling are only very small parts of why you should be investing. The important reason for doing this is for YOU. Are there things you want in life but feel you will never be able to afford? Are you worried about your future and how you will survive when you retire? Are you one of the majority of working people who cannot afford life insurance and, therefore, worry about your family if something should happen to you? Do you just want more out of your life?

Probably most people think at one time or another of owning their own business and, for one reason or another, never get around to doing it. Investing in the stock market is investing in a company and becoming part owner of it. You may feel that you do not have enough money to start your own business, but you have enough to invest in another business and take pride in watching that company grow and prosper and taking you right along with it.

What do you want from your life? How about buying your first home or a new, larger home? Or getting a college degree? Or even being able to retire at 45 instead of 65? If you are trying to save for your first home, you may be wondering whether owning a house is worth it if you have to save for twenty years just to get a minimum down payment. That in itself is a major problem because the smaller your down payment, the higher your monthly payment will be which will put even more stress on your small budget. Also, in today's market place, we all need to wonder whether investing in our own house is a good investment or will the value decrease below it's purchase price as has been happening in many areas of the country. But it does seem to be a natural instinct to want a place of our own. So do you think it would help if you could save all of the down payment you will need in 5 years instead of 10 years?

When you are in your twenties, you probably do not want to be tied down to a house and its payments, yet that is a good time to be saving for it. You might be reading this right now and saying to yourself, "I'm only 21 years old and plan on enjoying my freedom for quite awhile before settling down with a spouse, kids, and a house!" But even at 21 you can probably think of other things you would like to do. How about that trip around the world before you settle down or that Porsche? Or how about retiring at an early age?

The point is, you can and should invest in your future even if you do not have a clear goal. However, it is always much easier to save when you do have a clear goal to head for. It is a fact that it is almost impossible to accomplish anything in life if you have not already figured out what it is you want. So if you have to, just invent something in your mind that you want to save for. After all, there is no law against changing your mind in the future when you have enough money from your investments to do whatever you want to do. But it is important in anything, whether career, family life, or your personal life, to have goals you are headed toward. If you need help with figuring out "what you want to be when you grow up", creating those goals and sticking to them, read our book, *Building Your Dream Life: Career, Sex & Leisure.*

If you are in your thirties, do you want to go back to school or do you want to help your children go to college some day? You can actually start your children on saving the day they are born with just a few dollars a month in the stock market. Then when he or she is old enough to work part-time, they can be adding to that every month. The same goes for your own education Just because you cannot afford to go to college directly out of high school does not mean life is over. You can still have a successful career or start your own business, you can still marry and raise a wonderful and happy family without college. But if you start saving from every paycheck as soon as you get out of high school, you will be surprised at how quickly those few dollars will grow.

Do you want to live comfortably when you retire and/or be able to retire before age 65? That is probably the number one financial concern of people in their forties and upward. We know that the social security system was

15

created to help widows, orphans, and the older person survive retirement. It is important to remember that it was never meant to be the sole support of anyone. Therefore, it is up to each of us to take care of our own futures. Currently, 4.5% of your pay check goes into the social security system. If you make only $5 an hour, that is about $9 a week or $36 a month. Could you afford to save that much each month for your own use? Can you afford to save just 1% or $8 a month that will grow much faster than your social security deduction will?

You see, it does not take much to invest in yourself and, when you make your own investments, you are controlling it and do not have to worry about politicians using your money for something else or about the fund going bankrupt and losing all of your money. Then, if social security is still around when you retire, it will be what it was meant to be: an additional help in your retirement years, not your sole means of support. Let your government-controlled social security grow little by little but have your own investments grow 100% or more a year.

The point is, investing is a way to save for short-term as well as long-term things while remembering that short-term investing is riskier with a very high chance of losing money (we will discuss this fully later). A pension plan is a long-term investment because it is meant only for your retirement. But it comes with a sizable penalty if you withdraw **your** money early. And remember that, even with a pension plan, we are talking about **your** money, not someone else's. When we talk about saving using our method for long term things such as a downpayment on a home, we are talking about 5 to 10 years (but no less than 5 years). That may sound like a very long time to you but, compared to a pension plan, it is relatively a very short period of time.

Social scientists say we are living in a time when people have come to expect "instant gratification". Well, those social scientists know that there is no such thing as instant gratification - - everything takes time. You and I know that, too. However, even after we lecture you on not expecting instant gratification, it is very satisfying to have your own savings system in place whereby you can watch your money growing on a monthly basis and know that you are the one doing it. It may not be instant, but it is filled with gratification. And you will have only yourself to praise for doing it and, believe it or not, you can actually have fun saving for the future. After all, if you have a hobby of collecting something, say Christmas tree ornaments, it is fun seeing a new one added to your collection. Seeing your money increase in an easy and painless fashion can be just as satisfying. Maybe we should get rid of the word "saving money" and instead call it "collecting money"!

Should you invest to get rich? "The man who starts out simply with the idea of getting rich won't succeed; you must have a larger ambition." (John D. Rockefeller) The idea of Scrooge hoarding his gold is funny to us, but that is what happens when we invest just to become rich. Investing for your future is a much better ambition. And we would be willing to bet that if we asked you what you would like to do when you retire if money were no object, you could probably come up with some very interesting pursuits, and not one of those pursuits would be sitting all alone in a vault counting your money.

There was an interesting story we once heard about a typical couple who retired. He had worked hard at a blue-collar job all of his life. His wife had stayed home to raise the children and take care of their home. They had to pinch pennies, but they were happy. Then, when he retired at 65, his wife told him they had won a contest and the prize was something they had always dreamed of: an around the world cruise. They had a wonderful trip, but he was spending a great deal of time worrying about how they would survive when they got home now that he was retired as he had never made enough to save for their future. She finally told him that he did not have to worry any more, that they had not won the cruise, but that she had been saving just a few dollars each week out of the grocery money and investing it in the stock market. Now they were quite wealthy and he would not have to worry any more. Needless to say, he was very surprised but very happy.

Unlike some of the infomercials you see on TV, we are not talking about some get-rich-quick scheme. Nor do we have attractive people claiming how many thousands of dollars they made in a given time. We are talking about putting your money into secure investments that will provide you with a comfortable living realizing that "comfortable" can mean different things to different people. We are talking about security for your hard earned pay check. However, likewise, we cannot promise that you will not become rich. For some people, having investments worth $100,000 is rich while to others nothing short of a billion dollars is rich. Also, becoming "comfortable" or "rich" depends on whether you follow our method so as not to lose the money you have saved and whether you follow our steps and thus increase your savings each month. It also depends at what age you actually *start* investing. Remember, the earlier you start investing, the more wealth you can accumulate for your retirement.

We realize that it is much easier to read this book and say you are going to do it some day than it is to actually start doing it. If you begin saving when you are 50 years old, you will not be able to build up quite as much as you would if you started at 30. Likewise, by starting as teenagers at 13 years old, they will not only be assured of having a comfortable retirement but, in all probability, will be able to retire at a much younger age. What you need to ask yourself is, "Will $100,000 or more make a difference in my life?"

What we can promise you is that our method provides a safe way to increase your savings at a much faster rate than your savings account, mutual fund, pension plan, etc. ever will.

There are many places to put your money including stocks, bonds, Certificates of Deposit, treasury notes, real estate, mutual funds, pension plans, and others. But this book is devoted to investing SAFELY but with much better GROWTH then any of these other vehicles can provide. Later we will talk about all of these choices and each of their pros and cons, but our method uses only one possible investment. And what do we consider a safe place to put our money?

The stock market. The stock market?! Safe?! Are you kidding?! No, we are not kidding. But first, let's take a look at the pros and cons of other places to put your money.

4. Where Should You Invest

When choosing where you should place your life's savings, you will need to keep in mind certain factors such as how much money is required to get started, how safe is it, how fast will it grow. We are only considering some of the most common savings methods so that you can easily compare these systems with the stock market. Knowing that at this point you do not want to use all of your spare time working on your investments, we are not considering the many other savings options that require in-depth knowledge, huge fees, large initial investments, very high risk, etc.

Why do we invest in the stock market: **it has throughout history outperformed all other forms of investment, it can be very safe if done properly, it is within the limits of even a very tight budget, and it allows you to control exactly what happens to your money.** Compare the history of security, ease of use, and the amount of initial investment needed for each of the following with that of the stock market.

Savings Account

For our younger reading audience, there used to be a time when putting your money into a savings account was an excellent investment. When we were children, we never received lower than a 5% return on our savings and sometimes as much as 10%. Now our banks are very profitable to their Board of Directors but not to the public whose money they use to create that profitability for their owners. During a recession you can expect an interest rate of as little 1.5%. During the 90's with very good economic times, you could expect an interest rate of 6%. And be prepared to have service charges taken out of your account also. So although you can open a savings account with very little money, you also earn very little profit, and banks do have risk involved. Some of you may remember the large savings and loan failures back in the 1970's when banks were going bankrupt every day. As you do not read or hear much about bank closings in the news these days, you have a tendency to think of the bank as being the safest place to put your money. Unless you currently work in banking, you are probably unaware that at least one bank a week closes its doors even now. If you would like to learn more about what really goes on in banks, read Bobbie's novel "The Banker Chronicles" based on our own experiences in banking. You might want to consider investing in the banking industry but don't think of a savings account as a way to secure your future.

Also, keep in mind that with several investment instruments such as savings accounts and Certificates of Deposit, you are actually giving your money to someone to invest in the stock market for you. The difference is that you put your money into a regular savings account and get 2% interest on your money. At the same time, the bank is using your money to invest in several things such as mortgages and credit cards along with the stock market and getting as much as a 15% or more return and giving you that measly 2%. The banks attitude is that they are giving you the privilege of investing with them so that they can give you as little as possible and they can make as high a profit as possible. Instead, why not develop your own attitude of investing for yourself whereby you will get the highest possible return on your money. And always remember that when you do give a bank your money, you are allowing them the privilege of using your money to their benefit.

However, having said all of this, we confess that we will be using savings accounts in our method once in awhile, but in a very limited way. After all, everything has its proper place.

Certificates of Deposit

It is difficult to call Certificates of Deposit CD's any more as that is too easily confused with something that goes into your computer. But for the brevity of this book, we will be referring to Certificates of Deposit as CD's. And do not confuse this with the term we will use later of Certificates which means an actual certificate of stock ownership.

A CD is money that you choose to invest in a type of savings account that, because of the high initial investment and the fact that you cannot touch your money for a guaranteed amount of time, will give you a higher rate of return. Many banks have a minimum deposit of $500 or more along with a penalty for early withdrawal. If you have this much extra money sitting around that you do not know what to do with right now or you know you will need that money in just one year, then you might want to look into a CD after carefully comparing all of the possible interest rates as they vary widely from one institution to another. This is certainly a very safe place to invest your money. However, we are interested in investments that require a much smaller initial sum of money and will actually have a much higher rate of growth.

Real Estate, Gold, and Collectibles

Real estate can be very lucrative, but you can also quite literally lose your shirt in it. Whether or not real estate is a good investment is very dependent on the economic situation of the country and even the specific area of the country you are interested in at the time, and that situation can change very quickly. With today's housing market, even owning your own home is not necessarily as good an investment as it used to be. Nationwide recessions as well as ongoing regional recessions have taught us that the value of the house you buy can easily drop below what you paid for it and it can take as long as 10 years to get that value back, if ever.

Of course, the value of any investment, including the stock market, can also change very quickly. However, our major concern is that real estate is not "liquid". That is, if the real estate you have invested in does not seem to be doing well and you want to get out of it, or you suddenly need a great deal of money for an emergency, it can take a very long time to sell your property. Stocks can be sold as quickly as making a phone call. Therefore, even if you are aware that the value of your house or even the apartment building you bought is dropping, it is not always feasible to quickly sell such property. And while you are waiting for a buyer, you will be watching the value continue to drop. Also, even considering what you might hear on a late-night infomercial on TV, it is safe to say that it takes a little bit more than $25 a month to invest in real estate.

We consider gold and collectibles as one category with real estate because they are physical items that one collects. You buy up real estate expecting to either make a quick profit by selling it again at a higher price or make a small profit each month through rental. You buy gold and other collectibles with either the thought of making a long-term profit or just for the fun of it. People can collect anything of gold to see what it will be worth in the future the same as they can a Renoir painting or even

Barbie dolls. Any sort of collecting of items should be done with the understanding that you are doing it for the enjoyment of owning these things and fully understanding that it may never, at least in your life time, increase in value. With this in mind, remember that we want to invest our money to see actual real growth in a safe manner.

Mutual Funds

A mutual fund is a collection of different stocks and other investment types that you buy along with a group of other people. The idea is that by going in with other people, you can all afford to jump into investing in a bigger way and also meet their minimum investment requirements. Mutual funds are also discussed under Pension Plans (see below) as these as well as 401K's and IRA's are usually all forms of mutual funds.

Mutual funds were created by brokers in the 1970's when they realized that they could make a great deal more money in fees and expenses if they could get our very large middle class population to invest with them. Before that time period, it was pretty much only the rich who invested in the market. But if they could get 40 people to invest a minimum of $1,000 each in just one month, they make more money than if they have 40 people investing only $100 in a month. In other words, dealing with the small investor was not worth their time and effort because they were looking for a very large income from other people's money.

Why do you go to a broker for investment advice? Usually because you feel that they are experts in investing and know things that would be much to complicated for you to learn. As you will see by the end of this book, that is not true. Investing in the stock market is actually very simple as is making safe decisions by yourself. Please keep in mind that brokers are salespeople. Their job is to sell you something because they make their living from your fees and expenses. According to *The Wall Street Journal*, it is estimated that 90% of all the brokers in this country never invest their own money in the market. Another fact that most citizens do not know is that the federal law says that anyone who handles your money for you, such as banks, brokers, insurance agents, financial managers, etc. are allowed to accept money and/or stock in payment from a company to recommend that you buy their stock. Usually this does not occur with individual companies (unless it is a new start-up trying to get investors quicky) but the brokerages who own one of the thousands of mutual funds practice this a lot. In other words, you think this broker really feels that this particular mutal fund would be the best investment for you but they are recommending another only because they were paid to. It could even be a mutual fund owned by that brokerage you are talking about and, obviously, they are going to recommend their own. However, the law also states that they are supposed to tell you if this is happening. But quite often it is a matter of, if you don't ask, they don't tell. If you find yourself in this situation, stop and ask them how much they are being paid to recommend that you buy this fund.

Another problem with mutual funds is the required minimum initial investment. When funds first started, the amount was usually $5,000. Then during the 1990's as they wanted more people to invest with them, we saw the initial purchase dropping to $1,000 on average. However, when the country went into a recession and the brokerages were losing their fees and expenses income because investors had lost a lot of money and were pulling out of the market, the brokers raised this initial amount to $5,000 again. Now fewer and fewer brokers are willing to do the one share transaction that we will be talking about because they only want the big bucks.

With some mutual funds, you have a limited amount of control over which companies (or types of companies) you will be investing in and, in others, you have no control. The mutual fund buying and selling will be controlled by your broker to a greater or lesser extent. Again, you must answer the question of whether you want someone else making the decisions concerning your money and whether you are willing to spend a very small amount of time to handle your finances yourself in order to have control of the situation as well as save on the fees and expenses.

Keep in mind that when a broker or the company you work for gives you a choice of different types of mutual funds to get into, you do not really have a choice. That is, they will ask if you want to get into a retirement account or an income producing account or an educational account, etc. Research has found that no matter what they tell you, the fund you chose could be the wrong one. Let's say you want to get into a retirement account. This means you want a safe investment so you will be able to count on that money when you retire. But instead you find that you are in mostly high-risk investments with a very great chance of losing everything right down to your initial investment.

Do you know what you are invest in right now? To find out, contact the administrator of your account (ask your personnel office if it is through your employer), call them, and ask for a complete printout of everything you are invested in, not just the names of the funds you are in, but a break down of all of the companies each fund is currently in. You want to get this before the 15th of the month and not in the November/December period because, toward the end of the month and the end of the year, the broker will sell off stocks not doing well and buy up good looking stocks so that, by the end of the that period, they will have stocks in their portfolio that have been appreciating throughout the year. Now, brokers do not want you to have this information. In fact, according to USA Today, the Investment Company Institute general counsel stated, "There's no evidence that shareholders would benefit (from knowing where their money is invested)." Therefore, if they do not want to give you this printout, we suggest you tell them this is your money and you have the legal right to know what it is invested in.

Once you get this printout, see how many of the companies listed are large well-known companies, how many are foreign businesses (therefore highly risky), how many are high-tech (very risky), and how many names have you never heard of before (can be risky and you need to research those). How much of your future do you want tied up in very risky ventures?

Another problem with mutual funds is that you can research them and find one with an excellent track record, considering that excellent means up to 30% growth a year. But what will their track record be next year? If their record declines, you will need to be ready to make a change very quickly. The broker handling your investments may be excellent, but what will happen if there is a personnel change? Again, you will need to make a fast change.

Mutual Funds can give you more diversity in your investments more quickly in that you would have shares in over a hundred different companies. In fact, the average American mutual fund is invested in 130 different companies. The idea is that this will give you more safety. To check this out, let's go back to 1999, the last good year of the roaring '90's. At that time, it was reported that most mutual funds put 1/3 of your investment into very safe secure businesses (such as we will be talking about), 1/3 went into slightly risky investments, and 1/3 went into high risk companies (high-tech or startups). The idea was that if the high-risk companies flopped, you still had the safe ones so that you would at least break even. However, because you the owner were not checking this, the brokers changed this division. According to *The Wall Street Journal*, starting with the first quarter of 2000, of all the new money going into mutual funds, 90% was going into high-risk stocks. When the recession hit, it was inevitable that these funds were going to lose you a lot of money. But because you had a broker or administrator making these decisions for you, you had no choice. Please remember that we make our own choices in life. Would you ever tell your child to go out and find a complete stranger and give him or her all of their money? Of course you would not. Yet that is what you are doing every time you get into a mutual fund situation.

Also realize that for this diversity you are: (1) paying a management fee even when your investment loses value; (2) facing personnel changes that may make better or worse decisions for you; and (3) risking your money on a huge portfolio with some very risky stock involved that you have no choice over. Of course, for our purposes, the major problem (4) is that a minimum investment of at least $1,000 is usually necessary. At $25 a month it will take you over 3 years to save enough to start investing and that 3 years can be very discouraging. These high initial costs are why so many investment clubs have sprung up. Obviously, a group of people pooling their assets can meet the minimum dollar requirement and afford to jump into a mutual fund quickly (see below).

One other thing you should know about mutual funds is that you are usually paying monthly expenses but do not know it. According to Federal law, the only place you must be told about any monthly expenses is in your contract. Have you ever read your contract? Out of the thousands of attendees at our seminars, we have so far found only one man who said he had read his contract. We were shocked until he said that he was a lawyer. Well, this made sense so I asked him if he understood all of the brokerese in the contract. He hesitated several seconds before saying, "Well, most of it." Therefore, when you receive a statement from your broker saying your account is now worth so much, they have already taken out their monthly expenses but you never see it. But this is legal because it was stated in your contract. And if your broker tells you that there are no additional charges after your initial transaction fee, remember that no one does something for nothing.

Investing in one of the hundreds of Mutual Funds available takes a lot more research than the average person usually wants to do. To intelligently invest in a Mutual Fund, you need to fully understand front-end loaded funds (admission fee of as high as 8% plus the usual management fee when you open the account), back-end loaded funds (up to 8% fee when you sell plus the usual management fee), closed-end funds (you buy at a discount when it is offered but cannot sell unless they allow it and you still pay the management fee), and many other terms which seem to be increasing monthly. All of these different funds were created to make you think that you are getting a good deal such as, "Gee, I don't have to pay a fee until I sell when I can afford that 8% fee because all of my investments will have gone up!". But what happens if it has gone down? If you do not understand them, you can end up losing a great deal more than you put in originally.

Investment Clubs

Investment clubs have become quite famous in this country thanks to the Beardstown Ladies, a group of older women from the town of Beardstown, Illionois, some retired and some not, who formed a group to learn more about investing and to pool their money in order to meet the minimum investment (usually $1,000) required by brokers. They became famous because they were able to choose stocks and investments in which their return was much higher than the Standard & Poor 500 (S&P 500), a cumulative index of the best rated stocks on the market. Perhaps the major reason that the public thought this feat was worth a book about the Beardstown ladies is that it seemed amazing to some segments of our population that anyone, including women (and in this case, even elderly women) could learn how to build their financial portfolio and take care of their own money.

The ladies did eventually have a problem in that one of their members (not an accountant) had made some bookkeeping errors and it was reported to the media. The ladies apologized for having made the mistake but were still very concerned so they hired an accountant to do an audit of their books. It turned out that the main problem was that their bookkeeper had not taken into consideration the high fees they were paying their broker. Our point is that if you would like to form or join an investment club in order to share the experience of investing with others and not feel that you are all alone, this is still a good idea. But we recommend that each member do their own investing using our method so as to avoid those broker fees and any tax problems for members from pooling the money for investment.

We do not find it at all amazing that clubs usually do much better than brokers. After all, who cares more about your money, you or the broker? The secret to investing is to "learn" rather than depend on someone else. If you are not willing to learn, then you cannot do it. Knowledge gives you power, therefore, you should continually be learning new things, including how to increase your financial worth. Besides, isn't it fun watching your investments grow?

What do we dislike about a club? Do you really want to trust your money to other people? These co-authors own four businesses between the two of them; and yet, he has no partial ownership in her businesses and she has no partial ownership in his businesses. Why? Because too many good friendships (and marriages) have broken up due to joint business ventures. In a club situation, everyone votes on which investments to participate in and you must go along with the majority vote. How many of you are working for a boss who is making the wrong decisions for the company and there is nothing you can do about it? Do you want to get into that same kind of situation? When you are investing your own money, it is the same as having your own business. Therefore, you can and should make your own decisions. For some people, a club makes it easier to sit back and let others make decisions for you and thus, we suppose, to have someone else to blame for any mistakes made. However, we have found that clubs are having a problem with members dropping out because they do not like doing the calculations involved every month. If you are in a club having a problem with drop-outs, consider letting your math-fearing members use our method of research so as not to scare them away just because of numbers. And have each member do their own investing. Then you can compare with each other and gloat over how well yours is doing.

IRA's and Employee Pension Plans

First, remember that an IRA or pension plan is usually in the form of a mutual fund with wide diversification. The current maximum yearly amount you can put into your IRA (Individual Retirement Account) is at $4,500 (increasing to $6,000 in '08). As this is a maximum, you can open one for much less. If your budget allows for this, we encourage you to do so *if* you need to lower your taxes for the year. An IRA may not have the liquidity or the high growth of the stock market in that you will pay penalties for early withdrawal under age 59½, but it is a guaranteed source of income for retirement. Be aware that you are usually still putting your money into a mutual fund and will not have the growth we prefer.

You may work for a company that offers an employee pension plan such as a 401K plan. With this type of plan, you contribute a set amount from each pay check into a professionally managed fund. These plans allow you to defer or put off paying taxes in the year your money was earned while still earning interest on stock appreciation. A lot of people get into this type of plan, as well as other types, as a tax shelter. However, before doing this, we want to give you an example of how tax shelters work. Let's say that we offer to hand over to you, right now, a bag filled with $1,000,000 in cash. The only stipulation is that, if you accept it, you must immediately pay the IRS man 50% of it (realizing most income taxes are lower then that). Now you have to decide whether to accept the $1,000,000 knowing that you will only end up with $500,000 instead or turn us down. What do you do? You would accept it, of course, because half a million is better than nothing. The same is true with tax sheltered plans. With our method of investing you will make more money that you will someday have to pay taxes on. But even after the taxes, you will still have made a much bigger profit!

Sometimes your company will also contribute a set amount. If you are working for such a company, we usually suggest that you take advantage of this program. Whenever your employer matches what you put into your pension plan, you should join it as their share is just free money in your pocket and is part of your benefit package. However, always be aware of where the funds are being invested, i.e. stock market, mutual funds, etc. because then you need to read what we have said about each of those areas. Also, if your company is investing all of your money into their own business, as Enron did, do very careful research to make sure how your company is doing. The average investor with their limited knowledge might not have realized that Enron was in trouble long before you heard about it in the news. But if they had taken the time to do the research (we suggest reading *Adding To Your Financial Portfolio*), they would have found four signs showing that this was not a good investment. Having said that, also keep in mind that Enron was in a high-risk industry, which we do not recommend in this book as we are looking for safe secure investments.

If your pension fund is being invested in the company you work for, you need to be particularly carefully and research how well the company is doing. We suggest you follow the method we outline later in this book. However, since you are working in that area already, you will have additional places to research. For instance, if you are working in the banking industry and have the opportunity to invest in your particular bank, you will want to contact the public relations department for a copy of their annual report, talk to a senior vice president about the outlook for the company, call any contacts you have at other banks to chat about the banking industry as a whole (are they being bought out, are they closing any branches, are they laying off personnel). This will give you more insight into your industry, but you will still want to follow our suggested research to get totally unbiased opinions also. And if your employer is in a high-tech industry, please do the research found in *Adding To Your Financial Portfolio.*

After all, you are probably emotionally involved in your employment to the point that you would put your own money into a company that is not necessarily a good investment, or not as good an investment as you could otherwise make. Research your employer carefully along with other stocks in the same industry and compare it to other types of industries to decide where your money will do the best for you. Any information you can collect is only useful if you can determine its validity by comparing it with other information sources.

Stocks

But what we are talking about is investing in individual company stock. What would you say if we told you that historically the stock market has been the safest place in the world to put your money? This is actually true and we will prove it. In order to do this and for you to understand what is happening with your money, we are going to give you a little history lesson. You may not have enjoyed studying history in the past, but it is important for you to understand how the market works in order for you to trust in it as well as to make good investing decisions.

Following is a portion of a chart produced by The Value Line. We will talk about them later. This chart is called "A Long-Term Perspective of the Dow Jones Industrial Average". On this chart you will see three lines but the one we are interested is the one with vertical lines showing the high and low of the stock prices on a quarterly basis. That is, we are interested in knowing how the price of the stock has done.

This first section is from 1925 to 1936. You can see how the market had been climbing steadily until the big drop in October 1929 with the "Great Crash". You probably remember from your high school history that the crash lead us into a world wide depression. That is, this was not occuring in just the US but all over the world. You also remember your history teacher telling you that it lasted for 10 years and then World War II brought us out of it. However, if you look at the chart, you will see that the market started recovering after only 3 years, not 10 years. Why?

First, we have to know what the Dow Jones Industrial Average is. This is what you hear at the end of the day on the news as in how the Dow Jones did and that is what you and the government use to determine how the economy is doing. In the very early 1900's, the market (and the government) wanted a way to judge what any company should be capable of doing during any particular time period. That is, first

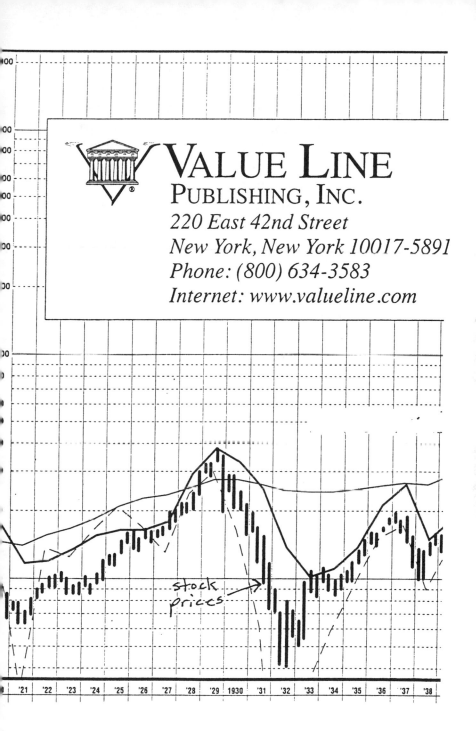

VALUE LINE
PUBLISHING, INC.
220 East 42nd Street
New York, New York 10017-5891
Phone: (800) 634-3583
Internet: www.valueline.com

stock prices →

'21 '22 '23 '24 '25 '26 '27 '28 '29 1930 '31 '32 '33 '34 '35 '36 '37 '38

41

they decided what the most important and essential industries in our country were. Back in 1920 the most important industry was railroads. Obviously, they are not too important today. In other words, the list of most important industries does change, very slowly, over time. Then from this list, they chose the 30 best performing businesses and that is what we judge our whole economy on. Does this seem fair? Why not use the average of all the businesses in the country? Actually, this method is very fair.

Let's say that you have a child in high school and he comes home with a D in his math class. Do you tell him, "That's okay. You can get all the D's you want." Probably not. You probably say something like, "What do you mean you got a D? Don't tell me it's the teachers fault. Other students are getting A's. You just need to work harder." That is, we want and expect our children to aim for the highest level of achievement possible. And we should want the same thing for ourselves. It would be very easy to use the average of what all companies, great ones and failing ones, do. But we do not want to strive for just average. After all, if these 30 companies are performing well and their stock is strong no matter what the current economic conditions, then why don't all the other companies in this country do as well? One of the main reasons is management. No matter how much financial backing a company has, they will not grow and earn profits unless they have good knowledgable management.

So we see in the chart that these 30 "good" companies suffered a great deal after the crash. But in just 3 years, we see their stock suddenly climbing very well while the other 99% of our businesses were still floundering. Why? Because these are the strong companies that recover quickly and will, therefore, keep your investment safe. When you own stock in a safe strong company and we go into a recession, all you have to do is sit back and wait till the recession is over and your stock goes right back up to where it was and continues to make money for you. By the way, although we have a recession on the average of once every 10 years, the average length of a recession since 1900 has been only 18 months.

Now let's look at another section of the chart from 1985 to the present. You will see a rather large drop in 1987 (October to be exact). On that day, the market dropped over 500 points in just one day. These days, we are used to the market dropping 250 points, going up 200 points the next day, dropping 200 points the next, going up 250 the next, etc. But in 1987, this was unbelievable. Investors panicked. They truly thought another great crash was happening. But in the chart you will see how quickly the market recovered (actually in less than two years). Why? To answer this, we first need to go back to 1929 and the Great Crash. At that time, people were allowed to invest on borrowed money. That is, they could put down

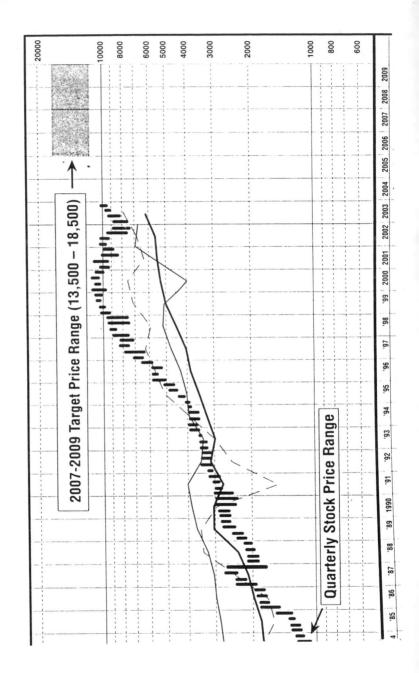

2007-2009 Target Price Range (13,500 – 18,500)

Quarterly Stock Price Range

44

10% and, if they had good credit, they could borrow the other 90% from their broker. They would sign a contract saying that on such-and-such a date they would sell this stock, pay back their broker, and make a good profit. This is called buying on margin. No one was worried because the 1920's had been a boom economy. The market had been soaring and even the media of the day said there was no reason for the market to ever slow down. It would just keep climbing forever. Sound familiar? That is why we now call the 1990's the "Roaring '90's" just like the "Roaring 20's".

We have a personal theory on this. It seems to be about 70 years between these huge market crashes. If the people who lost everything in 1929 were in their 20's, by the time the 1990's came roaring through, those people were now in there 90's. And who ever listens to a 90 year old person who is senile anyway? So for those of you who are quite young, remember this so that when you are 90 years old and the market is going wild again, you can warn everyone of what will eventually happen. Of course, no one will listen to you when you are 90, but you will have the satisfaction of saying, "I told you so."

The problem with investing on borrowed money was that when the crash occurred, those contracts came due, and they could not sell their stock for 10%, let alone what they owed their brokers. They lost everything. Well, the government immediately stepped in and changed the law so that an investor had to put 90% down and could borrow only 10%. But, as you are well aware, Congress has a tendency to change our laws and we don't pay attention until the deed is done. Currently, the law is at 50% down and 50% borrowed. However, be aware that in the past few years there have been certain individuals in Congress who have tried to change this law back to 10% down and 90% borrowed. So far it has not succeeded. But think of where we would be if they had changed that law. We had already gone into a normal recessional period when September 11th occurred. If the law had been changed, we would have found ourselves in a very severe depression. But because of the current law, the drop in 1987 did not have the severe consequences that 1929 did.

Now look at the last few years of the chart. You know that every October you can count on the market dropping. This happens because a lot of quarterly reports and year end predictions come out in October. Thus, starting on October 1st, you will see the brokers begin to worry and start selling and buying, madly trying to decide what is going to happen. Of course, no one knows what will happen. But brokers have a tendency to invest using only their emotions rather than their heads. However, on the chart you can barely see any fluctuation at all. Why? Another reason the stock market is becoming more and more stable is that we have more and more individuals like you and I investing directly in the market without going through brokers. The more this happens, the more stable our whole economy becomes. So, when you are done with this book, pass it along to your friends and relatives or anyone you do not want living off of you and social services in the future.

The stock market got quite a bit of bad press back in 1929. And yet, our method is based entirely on the stock market. Why? Because it is where you have the **greatest potential** for the **highest gains** and, if you follow our advice and use your own intelligence, you should have **very safe investments**. We could suggest a method that would have the potential for huge fast gains but would not be safe, and this we cannot condone for the beginning investor. We feel that the public needs to know about the great opportunities available through our stock market. You have as much right to increase your wealth as anyone else even if you are starting from a smaller base. It is only our individual greed that says, "it won't do me any good to invest just $25, it would take too long". Too long for what? Have you been given one month to live? It is greed speaking when you feel it is not worth it because you will only have $100,000 when you retire instead of $1,000,000. You are being sensible when you feel $100,000 is better than ending up with just social security (hopefully).

Learn from your past experiences as well as the experiences of others and **invest only in safe, secure, growth investments!** This is true of anything you invest in. After all, even banks can and do close their doors leaving your accounts (that are federally insured up to $100,000) to pay out only a fraction of what you had put in (currently averaging 90 cents on the dollar). And too many small businesses you are tempted to invest in go under because of trying to keep the company open after it has already stopped breathing! Finally, invest only what you can comfortably put away each week, because we personally know that there are lots of things to enjoy in life right now. You do not want to scrimp and save every penny just for retirement. You have to enjoy life now also.

We will be investing in **common stock** instead of preferred stock for several reasons. A business will only issue a limited number of shares of preferred stock, there is no reinvestment plan for it, usually no dividends are paid, and it will have limited growth as compared with common stock.

The purpose of this book is to increase your capital. However, having lived and worked all over this world, we are both very patriotic (we realize how old fashioned this sounds). We firmly believe in the capitalist system that gives us the right to start our own small businesses (90% of businesses in this country are five or fewer employees). As we both come from early pioneer stock, we also firmly believe in our lives only having a purpose if we are taking care of ourselves and then, with our success, helping the less fortunate. Thus, we would like to point out that when you invest your money to build your own capital, you are also helping the backbone of this country, private enterprise. When we are young and struggling, there seems to be nothing left to even help ourselves. Then, when we have learned a great deal more, we may not have a lot of money, but we have time to volunteer to help others. But eventually, through 90% hard work and 10% luck and intelligence, we have enough to share with others financially. So, help yourself and help your country and your neighbors by investing in the stock market and in American companies. Without our American companies, you would be out of work.

So why do we put all of our money into the stock market? First, the stock market has out-performed all of the other forms of investment since 1900 (yes, including the crash of 1929). Since 1929, the stock market has increased in value 3 out of every 5 years. The stock market is not gambling if you are investing in safe companies.

Second, remember that there are steps to follow in order to invest safely that we will be covering in great detail. If you decide not to follow these steps and start investing in riskier stocks with the hope of faster growth, you will be risking your own future. Learn from what happened in 1999 and make your own investment decisions. Historically the investor who sticks with safe investments (but that have large growth) has always made more money then the risk takers.

The third reason to invest in the stock market is that it is the one we can all afford. As the title of this book says, you can invest $25 or less every month and then sit back and watch your investment grow.

The fourth reason is actually a number of good reasons: the stock market allows you to choose your own investments thus giving you complete control of your money, you can actually become part owner of an established successful company, and it is fun.

Keep in mind that investing is legalized gambling. If you are already addicted to gambling, do not get into the market. You may need medical help to overcome this kind of compulsive illness. To invest wisely, you must invest with your head, not your heart. Occasionally you can invest using both your head and your heart, but not very often. One person we know decided to invest a few dollars in a new start-up company headed by a famous actor that she was very fond of. She purchased 10 shares at $17 the day this new company went public on the stock exchange. This stock never saw $17 again and has since closed.

Fortunately, she did not lose much but she now understands about using your head rather than your heart when you invest. However, we will now contradict ourselves.

Occasionally you can invest using both your head and your heart as when we invest in Disney. Its long term history is excellent (so our heads are satisfied) even if we did spend our honeymoon at Disney World (our hearts told us to do it). Actually, this demonstrates one of the best reasons for investing in any company and that is **invest in companies that you know and understand and use.** Besides being very familiar with the Disney movies, we know their parks (we visit every year), how they are kept clean, the great attitude of their employees, etc. If we had gone to a park and found it dirty and in disrepair, would we have invested in that company?

Shortly, you will learn the steps to doing safe growth investing without using a broker. You will learn how to develop your own investment plan that will give you a road map to carefully follow and to keep your emotions in check. Just like a road map, if you do not follow your financial plan, it will take you longer and cost you more to get where you want to go, if you get there at all. Developing a plan probably sounds very much like getting organized. Well, it is necessary to become at least a little organized. For some of you, that means, "Oh no, I can't do this, I'm totally disorganized." Don't panic. When we talk about being organized, we mean as in do you pay your bills every month. That's all. We have written our method of investing in book form and in step-by-step detail to make it easy for you.

Besides giving you the details of what to invest in and how to invest, we will be helping you with other areas directly connected to your financial plan. To develop your plan, you will need to decide how much you can invest each month and where to invest it.

You will be investing for the long-term or what you will have after 5, 10, 15, 20, or 30 years. You can only have safety in the stock market by investing long-term because you will be less likely to make mistakes caused by greed or fear. Greed can lead you to purchase stock trying to become instantly rich and fear can make you sell a safe investment and, thus, lose future earnings you would have had. We all must take chances in life, but we must learn how to take carefully researched chances that we know, in the long run, will succeed.

You may work for someone else right now but, when it comes to investing your money, you are working for yourself and you are the boss. Or, you decide to give your life over to someone else such as a stock broker or financial planner and thereby lose control of everything. As the boss, you must learn not to make decisions based on your fear of what the market might do tomorrow (no one can predict what tomorrow will bring anyway). People who are constantly buying and selling (referred to as day trading) are either trying to get rich quick or they are letting their doubts and emotions make their decisions. As we have already pointed out, if you are investing in safe companies, your stock will quickly regain whatever you might have lost during a brief downturn or even during a longer recession if you hold onto it and don't panic.

Do not watch the market every day. You will drive yourself nuts! You see your stock go up one dollar and wonder if you should sell it now before it drops again or should you buy more. Relax and enjoy the cozy feeling of knowing that your money is safe. And remember that slow and steady always wins the race. The point we are trying to make is that you can invest just a little each month in a safe company and still be following the rule of "buy low and sell high" because our method feeds into what is called "dollar cost averaging" and will be explained later. Buying and selling every few days or weekly is not fun and will just keep you from getting a good night's sleep besides becoming expensive with all those brokerage commissions.

If you find this book very interesting and want to learn more about the market and our economy, you might want to read *Adding To Your Financial Portfolio* in order to learn about making riskier investments. But that is only for those who have a true interest and a great deal more time to spend on investing.

You will be investing in stocks considered to be in the blue-chip category, that is, in large, healthy, growing companies that will still be around when your grandchildren are investing. However, please do not confuse our blue-chip list with the list the New York Stock Exchange considers "blue chip". It takes the market a long time, sometimes many years, to catch up with what is actually happening in the business world. Therefore, stocks that are extremely stable can take years or even decades to become an actual blue chip stock even though they have already reached that status in the real world. And it can also take years for businesses that are becoming passe (such as railroading) to be taken off the blue chip list. You will be developing your own list of blue chip stocks based on your own sound judgement and easy research.

When you buy stock in any business, you are buying a part of that company. You now own it. So, do you want to buy a get-rich-quick chance or a solid American business? We have all heard of the entrepreneurs who buy into a small start-up company and then one year later sell their stock at a huge profit to "get rich". If you feel like investing in a new business, start your own where you will have control and make the decisions. When investing in other companies, keep your money safe by investing in proven businesses.

Psychologists tell us that security is an ingrown need right after food and shelter. Therefore, we assume in this book that the vast majority of you want security both now and in the future. Generally speaking, the smaller the company is, the riskier the stock is. Also, any stock that sells at $10 or less (called penny stock) is usually extremely risky. It follows the saying, "You get what you pay for." Historically, the odds are extremely high that company will not make it.

Back in 1999, you were probably wishing you had invested in some of the technology stocks when they first came out. Of course, when a company goes IPO (initial public offering), there is no way to know what the future will bring. What you and I did know from government statistics is that 9 out of 10 new companies fail within the first 5 years. However, now as you look back you realize that you would have lost everything by investing in those businesses. And, hopefully, those of you who did decide to venture into the dangerous rapids of high-tech investing have learned your lesson well. It does no good to worry about the great investment that got away. You will do much better to concentrate on the future. Right now it would seem that MicroSoft can do not wrong, but what about 10 years from now? Keep in mind that there was a time when Apple

Computer could do no wrong but things changed. When there is a huge catastrope such as a world-wide financial collapse or even natural disasters such as hurricanes, floods, etc. how necessary will technology be in your life. If all the power and phone lines are down, will you be using your computer. Yes, those industries are in the process of making changes so that these industries will still be viable no matter what happens such as more and more communities getting underground wiring to protect our communications. But when a disaster occurs, we know that people are concerned with rebuilding their homes, finding grocery stores that are open and have food and water to buy. After a hurricane, schools are concerned with rebuilding and getting the basic supplies, not buying new computers. A business that has been physically ruined will be back in business quickly if they supply a necessity of life rather than the unnecessary things. We will be discussing the difference between the necessities or essentials of life that people always need and the other things in life that come and go depending on the situation later in this book.

Other countries have seen this type of destruction for many many years. Only recently, with the September 11th bombing, have you seen what happens after a huge disaster. And what you saw were companies, that were already well established and with good management, working out of their employees homes or quickly relocating to one of their other offices around the country. However, those businesses that were not stable and secure are no longer in business.

Let's play the "what if I had invested in one of those high-tech companies that first day its stock was released to the public" game. Back in 1971 a new company went public. At that time, no broker or financial magazine or newspaper would have recommended that you buy it because the company really didn't have anything tangible at that time. But, for whatever reason, you decided you really had to buy one share of stock in that company. So on opening day, you bought one share at $23. Now, let's say you put that share away in your drawer and just forgot about it for all these years. Then, after 30 plus years, you decided to do some house cleaning and found it. You took it to your CPA to find out how much that one share was now worth and he told you it was worth $915,000! Almost a million dollars! So what stock was that? It was Intel. But remember that at that time no one in their right mind would have bought that stock. In fact, most of the stock was bought by just a few employees who really had faith in their company. But also remember that for all the new companies that went public during that same year, less than 10% are still around today. All we are trying to point out is that until the day arrives that we literally cannot survive, as in live and not die, without technology, it is not an essential industry and, therefore, not safe and secure for our investing purposes.

Investing in these high-tech companies and brand new businesses is a very chancy game to play with your money. We will be teaching you how to find the success stories that you will not have to worry about whether from essential industries or non-essential.

Remember that one of your primary goals is to invest your money where it will grow to give you more wealth. According to numbers compiled in 1994 (before the boom and bust economy of the late 1990's), the Standard & Poor 500 showed a 9% return during the previous 25 years which is typical for normal times. During the same typical time period, that outperformed corporate bonds (4.4%), treasury bills (3.3%), and inflation (3.3%). Of course, you saw huge drops in your investments during the recession but, over the last 50 years, the safe secure stocks that have dropped have regained their original value in no more than 24 months as opposed to the risky stocks that may take many years to recover from a long recession. This means that in order to invest safely in the market, you must invest for the long haul so that you will not have to worry about how a recession or brief drop is effecting your portfolio. Plus, you actually save more money when buying in these long-term investments because you are not constantly buying and selling and creating more transaction fees.

One of the obvious savings in doing safe secure investing is cutting out these transactions fees that brokers charge for every purchase and sale. However, even using our method, you may occasionally be paying a one-time broker fee for an initial purchase or subsequent sale. Therefore, you want to be very sure that the stock you are holding is going to drop in price and continue to drop before you decide to sell it. Using our method, your portfolio will consist of stocks so strong that their value will always rise again. If you are having doubts about this, lets look at another example of how this works.

We all remember September 11th. You probably remember that the New York Stock Exchange closed immediately and did not reopen until the following Monday. Some of you may remember that on that day every single stock in the country went down (no exceptions). However, on the next day, Tuesday, a handful of stocks actually went up and the one that went up the most was Johnson & Johnson, an old well-established, strong and essential business.

One thing we hope you will find in this book is that investing can be fun and something you do not need to be an expert in. If you have to watch your portfolio every day to decide whether to buy or sell, the average person will not be having fun. Of course, there are some of you who do consider that to be fun but we are writing for the average citizen, just like ourselves, who consider traveling, snorkeling, hiking, going to the theatre and such as a lot more fun. Our method is for the person who does not want to become an expert in investing but who wants their money to be safe and secure for their future.

Statistically, ordinary citizens who invest in individual stocks rather than mutual fund situations have made better market decisions then the professional analysts and brokers have. That makes sense when you stop to think that you care more about your money than someone who is going to get paid whether he makes more money for you or loses your money. Even the best educated analysts and brokers who are honest and actually trying to help you make still make mistakes. Of course, the reputation of that entire field has suffered a great deal as you learned about the insider deals going on (that are illegal), the companies lying on their financials, and all of the other fallout as Americans have decided to watch businesses more carefully after what Enron did. However, even without the actual law breaking, brokers not only make mistakes but then double them by insisting on buying and selling continually in order to earn more expense fees for themselves.

Although neither of the authors has ever worked as a broker or analyst, Bobbie did work as a secretary for a large brokerage firm in Boston many years ago. Although she was not then involved in her own investing, it seemed amazing to her at the time that, even when the broker invested unwisely so that a person lost not only what money had earned but even lost their initial investment, that person still had to pay the broker's fee every month. In other words, the broker makes his money whether he makes a good decision for you or not. This is why most mutual fund situations (including your pension fund) are continually changing their makeup; that broker only makes fees when they buy or sell stock for you.

If you think that you need a Ph.D. in order to invest your own money, let me ask you how many rich Ph.D.'s do you know? Besides, as Ben Franklin, the creator of the first public library knew, you can learn anything you want or need to know at your library. In fact, all of the research we will be talking about can be done for free at the library. Even if you find yourself really enjoying the complexities of the stock market and want to become an expert in it, you can get all the advice and knowledge of the very best experts from the books those experts have written at your library. But also keep in mind that we live in a free country and anyone can write a book. Before believing an expert, stop and think about what they are trying to sell you. Is that book written by or that seminar given by a broker or financial manager (a new euphemism for broker) who wants you to believe that the market and investing is so complicated that you must go to them for help?

After reading this book, you will never need to depend on your local broker's opinion again.

For that matter, do not depend on and trust anyone else's opinion either. You would be amazed at how many of yor friends and relatives will be more then willing to offer their advice on investing your money. But you must always consider whether they actually know what they are talking about or not. You may have a sister who works as a bank teller, but that does not make her an expert on banking unless she has gone out of her way to become an expert on it. Has she done extensive research on the banking industry and what outside places is she getting her facts from? If she is quoting The Wall Street Journal, you may want to follow up her research with your own to see if this particular bank is a good investment.

But it is not necessary to be an expert with a complicated system to succeed in the stock market. You will find this method to be very simple and takes very little time. You can spend as little as a couple of hours to make a good investment decision or, if you find it more interesting than you thought it would be, you can spend lots of time on it.

A lot of people consider brokers to be experts but how many rich stock brokers have you known? They may try to have the outer signs that they are well to do but looks can be very deceiving. If they are rich, why do they work so hard to get your money? And the stock market itself is not that complicated. If you want to start a company and need money to buy a building and supplies, then you look for investors. Once you have that business established and want to expand your company, you again look for investors. That is what the stock market is about. The system of buying and selling on the floor of the New York Stock Exchange is very confusing, almost seeming to verge on mayhem. But you do not have to get involved with that mayhem. However, if you are going to be in New York, the stock exchange does give very interesting tours.

The fact remains that no one is more interested in your money then you are! Well, with the possible exception of Uncle Sam and, as you get older, your children. You have worked hard to earn your money and you should be the one making decisions on how to invest your money. Trusting someone else to do what is best for you is never a good idea in any part of your life and definitely not a good idea when it comes to your future survival and comfort.

So, in answer to the original question, what should you invest in in order to have safe low-cost investments that you will not have to constantly watch and worry about, **you are going to learn how to find the large, well-known, growing companies that will increase your investment quickly and safely plus save money by not using a stock broker.**

Everyone who has played Monopoly knows it takes money to make money. So can you be successful without having a big bankroll? As William J. O'Neil said, "Success in a free country is simple. Get a job, get an education, and learn to save and invest wisely." Hopefully, you already have the job and the education (if not, order *Building Your Dream Life*) and now we will give you the knowledge you need to save and invest wisely.

O'Neil also said that in his experience "a person's years and quality of education have very little to do with making money investing in the market." And he is right - - even children can learn to invest and some of the most successful investors in history never even graduated from high school. However, we feel he left out another very important point. It also does not matter whether you are a man or a woman, what your background is, where your family comes from, or what your religion is. When it comes to investing our own money, we are all created equal and there is no "glass ceiling" on your potential. Women can invest as wisely as men and you do not need your spouse's permission to invest your own money. Our country is supposed to be a free enterprise society and, when it comes to investing, it really is.

Of course, if you never take that first step because you don't believe you can be successful, then we can guarantee you that you will not be.

We know that getting past any remaining doubts and actually taking that first step is the hardest one in the world, but we hope that this book will give you an easy plan to follow and will reduce the fears you may now have until you actually see your money growing and then you can teach others how to do the same thing. We know that you can do it because we have done it.

5. How Much Can You Save Each Month

The number one excuse people use for not investing is that they have nothing left at the end of the month after paying all the bills. There are obvious solutions to this such as taking on a part-time second job (the co-author once worked three jobs at one time, however, she was single at the time). But usually you do not need more money than you currently have in order to start investing.

An often overlooked fact is that even very good stocks can sell for as little as a few dollars up to over a hundred dollars per share. We are not talking about penny stocks that are here today and gone tomorrow but rather only good safe investments. But the price of a share of stock, in even a huge company like Johnson & Johnson, can vary from $40 to $150 a share, give or take a few dollars. In fact, even during this recession, we saw its stock price fall to $41 a share. However, for now, all you need to know is that you will need about $100 to get started. "Wait a minute!!! You said I only needed $25 or less a month to invest!!" We are talking about $25 a month and that is what we will stick to. That is, when you buy stock in any company you must buy at least one whole share to get started and can then mail in a smaller amount each month which we will go into in more detail shortly. However, when talking about starting with about $100, remember that you can always put your $25 a month away in the good old savings account until you have that $100 for the first purchase. So, in abbreviated for, our method is this:

You only need to invest in <u>one</u> share of stock (let's say about $40 worth) to get started and then invest $25 a month (or less) which, along with reinvestment of dividends and splits, will keep your money growing.

We have given you one example using Johnson & Johnson but here is another, longer term example. Let's say your grandfather bought one share of General Electric back in 1892. Since then the gentleman has passed away and you inherited everything. In sorting out his belongings you happen to come across this stock certificate. You take it into your CPA and you find out that this one share is now worth over 152,144 shares worth approximately $3.3 million today. And he never added any more money to this account after buying just that one share.

On the cover of this book, it is clearly stated "on $25 a month (or less)". We picked $25 because it seemed like an average amount that most people could afford. But the method we are going to be talking about can be used for any monthly dollar amount whether you can afford $10 a month or $200 a month. Only you can decide how much that monthly dollar amount should be. The examples we will be using in this book are all based on $25 for comparisons sake. However, if you are a student mowing lawns or a single parent working two jobs, you can still use this method but at a lower monthly amount, even only $10 a month. For instance, General Electric requires that future purchases be for at least $25. But General Foods will accept as little as $10. You see, the rate or percent at which your money grows will be the same no matter how much you are contributing; it just may take a little longer to get where you want to go. But you will get there! If you invest in a strong, safe company that is showing its investors a 30% annual growth rate, you will get that 30% whether you are investing $25 a month or $200 a month. In other words, it may take you longer, but you are being treated exactly the same as everyone else. And, yes, this method works for those of you have more money to invest each month. If you are sending in $100 a month instead of $25, your portfolio will grow bigger faster.

It does not matter whether you are investing $10 a month or $200 a month. What is important is that you invest the same amount each month because we are talking about a regular monthly savings plan. I can remember years ago setting up a Christmas Savings Account so I would have enough to buy presents for the holiday. But guess what? It seemed that each week (or month) I just did not have that $10 to put into the bank. Thus, the first (and only) rule of saving, which you have probably heard many times, is **pay yourself first**. No one else is going to take care of your finances, nor should they. Only you can save your own money for your own future. Later we will talk about how easy it is to pay yourself first using this method.

In order to decide what your monthly amount is going to be, you need to go over your budget and see how much you can afford to invest each month (not weekly) without going hungry. Go through your check book for the past six months and add up all the checks you wrote. Then go back through the check book again and add in all of those ATM withdrawals. Now add these all up and divide by six to get an average amount you are spending each month. Compare this amount with your paycheck. You should find that you are making more then you are spending. If you find it is the other way around, you might want to read *Building Your Debt-Free Life* first. But most of you should have a little bit left over and this is what you want to plan on investing each month. After all, if you just cut out one family meal at McDonald's each month, you would have saved enough money to get started.

For ease in understanding, we will refer to $25 a month throughout this book even though you may have a different amount in mind. In order to use this method correctly and to **build** your financial portfolio, you must treat this $25 as a regular monthly bill. We will show you a way to make sure you pay yourself first every month a little later.

We told you this method of investing does not take a lot of your time. Therefore, after you have started your investment plan, pick one day a year (we suggest on New Years Day), to go over your budget and see if you can increase this amount. If your family budget will not tolerate an increase, that's okay. And if an emergency comes up, its okay to cut your monthly amount back. However, if you must cut back, do not tell yourself it will only be this once. Instead, cut back to $10, or whatever you can **easily** save out each month, until you are sure you can safely increase to $25 again. And do not increase your monthly amount unless you are sure that, for the foreseeable future at least, you will be able to maintain that monthly amount. We want you to enjoy your investing so choose a monthly amount that will work well for you, not an amount that will be too difficult for you. We have found that being **consistent** is very important in creating your monthly savings habit. If you get used to paying yourself each month, it will soon be a habit that you will not even think about. So pay yourself first.

6. How To Find The Right Stock

Basically, our method is picking out **what** stock to invest in. Note that we said stock, not stocks. We all know the expression "don't put all your eggs in one basket", however, we also feel that one egg is better than no eggs!

Which company should you invest in? You want it to be safe to protect your savings but you also want it to be growing so that you do not have to do all the work. If it doesn't grow, you might as well keep your money in a savings account or under your mattress!

To determine which stock is right for you, we need to do a little research. Don't panic! We said **a little**. You do not need to become an expert in the stock market to invest in it. And you do not need to spend a lot of time. You can spend a few minutes at the library and pick out your first stock or you can spend a week. But, again, this book is meant for people who do not find investing all that interesting (only the resulting increase in your money is exciting) and want to spend as little time as possible doing research. In fact, reading this book or taking the seminar takes much longer then the whole method from start to finish takes in real life.

Now you are going to follow these steps to find safe, secure, growth investments.

1. Gut Instinct. "Gut instinct??!! How can I use gut instinct on something I know nothing about??!!" Don't underestimate yourself! You know more about the market than you think you do.

For instance, do you remember the Yugo car? Did you buy one? Probably not as very few people did. So, *who* decided the Yugo car would go out of business? You did! You didn't buy one. If you do not buy a company's products and/or services, they will go bankrupt. You and I, the American consumers, do 60% of all purchasing in this country. That is more than all the largest corporations combined. So you are the ones who decide whether a company survives or not. Therefore, you control our economy.

First, take a piece of paper and divide it down the center. At the top of the left hand column write "essential" and at the top of the right hand column write "non-essential". That is, we need to figure out what are the truly essential industries that we always need no matter what happens.

There are currently 98 industries in this country. But very few are really essential. Let's go over some of the ones you might be thinking of right now.

Hopefully, the first thing you thought of was food and drink. Without these industries, you would be dead and it wouldn't matter what you invested in! When we say food, however, we are not talking about commodities. Commodities are the buying and selling of things like wheat, pork bellies, etc. Getting into commodities is extremely risky because you are basically betting against God. That is, will the crop be great this year or will there be a flood or a drought or any number of other things that can affect the crop. We never bet against God. To us food means the businesses that sell directly to grocery stores, restaurants, schools, etc. You may have noticed that we also said drink and not water. Yes, water is in everything to a greater or lesser extent. But if you were out in the middle of the desert and dying of thirst, would you turn down a beer (or something else you might not like to drink under normal circumstances) just because it wasn't water? No, you would not. The need to survive is built in and you would drink whatever was available. Therefore, any company that makes a beverage must be considered essential.

Did you think of power, utilities, electricity? You may think of power as being essential but it is not. Wherever you live there are some sort of weather conditions that can effect your power supply. We originally came from Maine and can well remember one storm that took out our electricity for five days. When something like this happens, do you all roll over and die? No. You learn to make do with what you have. You learn how to build a fire in that fireplace you have never used to keep you warm and to cook meals with. Because of this, electricity is not consider an essential industry. However, we will be using it later in connection with something else.

What about transportation? Most of you must have a car to get to work. And what about the trucking industry that supplies our grocery stores with food and our businesses with supplies? You have probably heard on news reports how many new cars were bought last month as an indication of how our economy is doing (are you spending enough to keep the economy growing well). But if we go into a recession and you do not know if you will have a job next month, do you go out and buy a new car? Does the trucking business go out and buy new trucks? No, usually you are sensible and decide to wait until you are sure of your future income. But you still need to get to work and produce and such has to keep moving. So what two things do you always need in order to keep the old cars and trucks running? You must have the oil products (gas, oil, etc.) and parts (brakes, engines, tires, etc.). Therefore, it is not the big industry that is the essential one but rather these sub-industries that we must always have.

The same thing is true of housing. You must have a place to live. You hear in the news how many new homes were built last month. But if you are not sure of your job security, you probably do not go out and buy a new home. However, just like cars, trucks, our bodies, and everything else, houses do slowly disintegrate. We have to keep them in repair. If you woke up one morning to find the rain coming through the ceiling of your bedroom, you might call someone to come and put a new roof on your house for a couple of thousand dollars. However, if you don't have that kind of money and don't know if you will be working next month, where could you go to find out how to do these repairs yourself and buy the necessary materials? In other words, it is not the housing industry that is essential. It is this sub-industry of home repair that we always have to have. If times are good, you might build a gazebo. But when times are bad, you still need to keep your house from falling down.

Hopefully, none of you thought of computers. Believe it or not, the world will not come to a stand still if all the computers in the world crashed, died, and never came back. Yes, it would be inconvenient, but life goes on. If you work for Ford Motor Company, would they go out of business if all the computers died? No, but they would have to hire a lot more people to do all the things the computers used to do. An accounting firm would have to go back to writing everything on spread sheets. Even the computer based companies would just switch to something else. In fact, we saw an example of that in 1999. You might remember a lot of media hype that year about how you were going to lose everything because the computers were not made to handle the year 2000. You would enter 00 and the computer would think you meant 1900. Actually, the banking business did not worry about this at all because they had already gone through the law change allowing intrastate banking. As big banks bought up small banks, they had to change their computer systems to match totally different systems so they had this down to a science. However, a lot of consultants made a lot of money living off this scare tactic created by the media. Because of this, high-tech industries such as computers, software, and telecommunications are not essential industries. Then why do so many people and the market consider phone companies to be safe? They used to be. For one thing, there was not as much competition back when AT+T was the one giant that made sure your calls went through. But something happened recently to AT+T as well as the other communications companies. They went high-tech. Now these companies are involved in broad band, satellites, etc. causing the market to change their name to telecommunications and making them high risk investments.

Did you think of pharmaceuticals? We certainly need these drugs today but it is important to remember that there are essential pharmaceuticals and non-essential ones. The essential companies are the ones making things we always have to have such as penicilin, aspirin, etc. However, when you find one that is putting most or all of its money into research, that is a high-tech business and, therefore, a high risk company.

Some people think of education as being essential. If you believe that, remember that our country was built by mostly uneducated people. Even today, according to the Department of Labor, the majority of successful small businesses (as opposed to unsuccessful) are owned and operated by people without a college degree with a full 35% of those being high school drop-outs. Visit any country currently in a war situation and you will find that education has virtually vanished.

We have already determined that you, the consumer, are the one who runs our economy. Therefore, you need to think of what companies or products you always have to have. For instance, if we ask you what toothpaste you buy, some of you might say Colgate and some might say Crest. And some of you buy whatever is on sale because the brand of toothpaste just does not matter to you. So think of those names that are important to you and put them under either the essential or non-essential column. This may take some people just minutes to do and some people could take a few days to complete their list. But when you are done, you need to use your essential list first. You will be using the non-essential part later.

By the way, if you want to list a particular brand but do not know what company makes it, there are several ways to find out. You can go online using the search engine Google and just type in the brand name to get that information. Or you can quite often just check on the package for the parent company. Or call your reference librarian and they can check for you.

In order to make life easier for you, you now want to choose just two or three of the companies listed under essential. You will take these two or three companies and go to the next step.

2. Research. You could research every company you have listed if you want but, again, we will assume you are not thrilled with the thought of doing research. We have found through our seminars that the number of people who really love doing research is extremely tiny as in one out of every 30 individuals. The good news is that because you are dealing with usually well-known companies, the research will be very easy.

You are going to go to your nearest library and use the *Value Line's Investment Survey*. If you really do not want to go to the library, you can purchase a subscription to the Value Line for over $500 a year. Or you can subscribe to their online service for over $600 a year (no paper or postage but more expensive!). As you will only be using this for a few minutes, we recommend you find your nearest library. Remember also that you can make copies at the library of the pages you want to study further.

You will find the *Value Line* in the reference section in a big thick binder. The *Value Line* comes out once a week. On the front cover of each issue they list several industries that they will be covering in that particular issue. Each week they will cover different industries so it takes about three months for it to circle around to the beginning again. Below each industry heading are listed the most commonly traded companies.

Following you will find a sample page from the *Value Line* that we will use as an example of how to read it and use the information. Although we have had to halve the size to fit this book, even full size it is still in very small print because they have to squeeze a lot of information onto that one page. Before you panic, you will only be using part of this information. It is not as difficult as it looks to you right now.

We are using Johnson & Johnson again as our example. What do you need to use on this page and what can you ignore.

In the upper left corner is an item called SAFETY and, for Johnson & Johnson (hereafter referred to as J&J), it is listed as "1" (or very

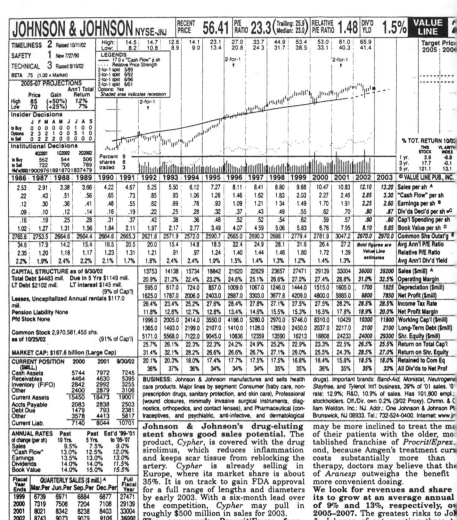

JOHNSON & JOHNSON NYSE-JNJ

| RECENT PRICE | 56.41 | P/E RATIO | 23.3 | (Trailing: 25.9) (Median: 23.0) | RELATIVE P/E RATIO | 1.48 | DIV'D YLD | 1.5% | VALUE LINE |

TIMELINESS 2 Raised 10/11/02
SAFETY 1 New 7/27/90
TECHNICAL 3 Raised 8/16/02
BETA .75 (1.00 = Market)

2005-07 PROJECTIONS
	Price	Gain	Ann'l Total Return
High	85	(+50%)	12%
Low	70	(+25%)	7%

Insider Decisions
	J	F	M	A	M	J	J	A	S
to Buy	0	0	0	0	0	1	0	0	
Options	2	3	2	1	0	0	5	1	0
to Sell	0	2	2	2	0	0	0	0	

Institutional Decisions
	4Q2001	1Q2002	2Q2002
to Buy	552	544	506
to Sell	722	706	789
Hld's(000)	1900976	1891870	1837479

LEGENDS
17.0 x "Cash Flow" p sh
Relative Price Strength
2-for-1 split 5/89
2-for-1 split 6/92
2-for-1 split 6/96
2-for-1 split 6/01
Options: Yes
Shaded area indicates recession

% TOT. RETURN 10/02
	THIS STOCK	VL ARITH INDEX
1 yr.	2.8	-8.8
3 yr.	17.7	-0.1
5 yr.	121.1	13.1

© VALUE LINE PUB., INC.

	1986	1987	1988	1989	1990	1991	1992	1993	1994	1995	1996	1997	1998	1999	2000	2001	2002	2003	
Sales per sh A	2.53	2.91	3.38	3.66	4.22	4.67	5.25	5.50	6.12	7.27	8.11	8.41	8.80	9.88	10.47	10.83	12.10	13.20	
"Cash Flow" per sh	.22	.43	.51	.56	.65	.73	.85	.93	1.06	1.26	1.46	1.62	1.83	2.03	2.27	2.46	2.85	3.30	
Earnings per sh B	.12	.30	.36	.41	.48	.55	.62	.69	.78	.93	1.09	1.21	1.34	1.49	1.70	1.91	2.25	2.60	
Div'ds Decl'd per sh ■C	.09	.10	.12	.14	.16	.19	.22	.25	.28	.32	.37	.43	.49	.55	.62	.70	.80	.87	
Cap'l Spending per sh D	.16	.19	.25	.28	.31	.37	.42	.38	.36	.48	.52	.52	.54	.62	.59	.57	.60	.60	
Book Value per sh D	1.02	1.27	1.31	1.56	1.84	2.11	1.97	2.17	2.77	3.49	4.07	4.59	5.06	5.83	6.76	7.95	8.10	9.85	
Common Shs Outst'g E	2765.6	2753.5	2664.6	2664.4	2664.6	2665.3	2621.6	2571.9	2572.0	2590.7	2665.0	2690.3	2688.1	2779.4	2781.9	3047.2	2970.0	2970.0	
Avg Ann'l P/E Ratio	34.6	17.9	14.2	15.4	16.5	20.5	20.0	15.4	14.8	18.5	22.4	24.9	28.1	31.6	26.4	27.2	Bold figures are Value Line estimates		
Relative P/E Ratio	2.35	1.20	1.18	1.17	1.23	1.31	1.21	.91	.97	1.24	1.40	1.44	1.46	1.80	1.72	1.39			
Avg Ann'l Div'd Yield	2.2%	1.9%	2.4%	2.2%	2.1%	1.7%	1.8%	2.4%	2.4%	1.9%	1.5%	1.4%	1.3%	1.2%	1.4%	1.3%			

CAPITAL STRUCTURE as of 9/30/02
Total Debt $4483 mill. Due in 5 Yrs $1149 mill.
LT Debt $2102 mill. LT Interest $145 mill.
(9% of Cap'l)
Leases, Uncapitalized Annual rentals $117.0 mill.
Pension Liability None
Pfd Stock None

Common Stock 2,970,581,455 shs.
as of 10/25/02 (91% of Cap'l)

MARKET CAP: $167.6 billion (Large Cap)

CURRENT POSITION	2000	2001	9/30/02
Cash Assets	5744	7972	7245
Receivables	4464	4630	5395
Inventory (FIFO)	2842	2992	3255
Other	2400	2879	3106
Current Assets	15450	18473	19001
Accts Payable	2083	2838	2503
Debt Due	1479	793	2381
Other	3578	4413	5817
Current Liab.	7140	8044	10701

ANNUAL RATES	Past 10 Yrs.	Past 5 Yrs.	Est'd '99-'01 to '05-'07
of change (per sh)			
Sales	9.5%	7.5%	9.0%
"Cash Flow"	13.0%	12.5%	12.0%
Earnings	13.5%	13.0%	13.0%
Dividends	14.0%	14.0%	11.5%
Book Value	14.0%	15.0%	15.5%

Fiscal Year Ends	QUARTERLY SALES ($ mill.) A				Full Fiscal Year
	Mar.Per	Jun.Per	Sep.Per	Dec.Per	
1999	6739	6971	6884	6877	27471
2000	7319	7508	7204	7108	29139
2001	8021	8342	8238	8403	33004
2002	8743	9073	9079	9105	36000
2003	9600	10000	10400	9200	39200

Fiscal Year Ends	EARNINGS PER SHARE A B				Full Fiscal Year
	Mar.Per	Jun.Per	Sep.Per	Dec.Per	
1999	.41	.41	.39	.28	1.49
2000	.47	.47	.45	.31	1.70
2001	.50	.51	.50	.40	1.91
2002	.59	.60	.60	.46	2.25
2003	.67	.69	.67	.57	2.60

Calendar	QUARTERLY DIVIDENDS PAID C■				Full Year
	Mar.31	Jun.30	Sep.30	Dec.31	
1998	.11	.125	.125	.125	.49
1999	.125	.14	.14	.14	.55
2000	.14	-.16	.16	.16	.62
2001	.16	.18	.18	.18	.70
2002	.18	.205	.205		

	13753	14138	15734	18842	21620	22629	23657	27471	29139	33004	36000	39200	Sales ($mill) A
Operating Margin	20.9%	21.3%	22.4%	23.2%	24.6%	25.1%	26.6%	27.0%	27.4%	28.8%	31.0%	32.5%	
Depreciation ($mill)	595.0	617.0	724.0	857.0	1009.0	1067.0	1246.0	1444.0	1515.0	1605.0	1700	1925	
Net Profit ($mill)	1625.0	1787.0	2006.0	2403.0	2887.0	3303.0	3677.6	4209.0	4800.0	5885.0	6800	7850	
Income Tax Rate	26.4%	23.4%	25.2%	27.6%	28.4%	27.8%	27.1%	27.5%	27.5%	28.2%	28.5%	28.5%	
Net Profit Margin	11.8%	12.6%	12.7%	12.8%	13.4%	14.6%	15.5%	15.3%	16.5%	17.8%	18.9%	20.0%	
Working Cap'l ($mill)	1996.0	2005.0	2414.0	3550.0	4186.0	5280.0	2970.0	5746.0	8310.0	10429	10300	11800	
Long-Term Debt ($mill)	1365.0	1493.0	2199.0	2107.0	1410.0	1126.0	1269.0	2450.0	2037.0	2217.0	2100	2100	
Shr. Equity ($mill)	5171.0	5568.0	7122.0	9045.0	10836	12359	13590	16213	18808	24233	24000	29300	
Return on Total Cap'l	25.7%	26.1%	23.3%	22.3%	24.2%	24.9%	25.2%	22.9%	23.3%	22.5%	26.5%	25.5%	
Return on Shr. Equity	31.4%	32.1%	28.2%	26.6%	26.6%	26.7%	27.1%	26.0%	25.5%	24.3%	28.5%	27.0%	
Retained to Com Eq	20.1%	20.3%	18.0%	17.4%	17.7%	17.5%	17.5%	16.8%	16.4%	15.8%	18.5%	18.0%	
All Div'ds to Net Prof	36%	37%	36%	34%	34%	34%	34%	35%	35%	36%	35%	33%	

BUSINESS: Johnson & Johnson manufactures and sells health care products. Major lines by segment: Consumer (baby care, non-prescription drugs, sanitary protection, and skin care), Professional (wound closures, minimally invasive surgical instruments, diagnostics, orthopedics, and contact lenses), and Pharmaceutical (contraceptives, and psychiatric, anti-infective, and dermatological drugs). Important brands: Band-Aid, Monistat, Neutrogena, Stayfree, and Tylenol. Int'l business, 39% of '01 sales. '01 depreciation rate: 12.9%; R&D, 10.9% of sales. Has 101,800 empl.; stockholders. Off./Dir. own 0.2% (3/02 Proxy). Chrmn. & CEO: William Weldon. Inc.: NJ. Addr.: One Johnson & Johnson Pl., New Brunswick, NJ 08933. Tel.: 732-524-0400. Internet: www.jnj.com.

Johnson & Johnson's drug-eluting stent shows good sales potential. The product, Cypher, which is covered with the drug sirolimus, reduces inflammation and keeps scar tissue from reblocking the artery. Cypher is already selling in Europe, where its market share is about 35%. It's on track to gain FDA approval for a full range of lengths and diameters by early 2003. With a six-month lead over the competition, Cypher may pull in roughly $500 million in sales for 2003.

The company's Procrit/Eprex franchise should grow roughly 7% in worldwide sales next year, to about $3.9 billion. Although Amgen's next-generation competitor for treating anemia, Aranesp, is a looming threat to Johnson & Johnson, the erosion of Procrit/Eprex sales will likely not gain much momentum until 2004 for several reasons. First, many oncologists are waiting for the outcome of ongoing dosing trials of Aranesp, which should be completed by early 2003. Also, the National Institutes of Health is planning a trial to investigate optimal dosing regimens of Aranesp and Procrit/Eprex. Until these outcomes are disclosed, doctors may be more inclined to treat the majority of their patients with the older, more established franchise of Procrit/Eprex. Second, because Amgen's treatment currently costs substantially more than this therapy, doctors may believe that the convenience of Aranesp outweighs the benefit of more convenient dosing.

We look for revenues and share net to grow at an average annual rate of 9% and 13%, respectively, over 2005-2007. The greatest risks to Johnson & Johnson of not meeting these targets would be delay in U.S. market clearance for Cypher, and Aranesp stealing market share away from Procrit/Eprex more quickly than we expect.

Although timely, this stock holds subpar total-return potential for the 5-year pull, as the issue recently bounced back strongly from a recent low of $41.40.

Nancy Chow   December 6, 2002

Sales (and Operating Margins) by Business Line			
	1999	2000	2001
Consumer	6864 (10.0%)	6904 (12.6%)	6962 (14.3%)
Professional	9913 (16.5%)	10281 (16.5%)	11191 (17.9%)
Pharmaceutical	10694 (34.9%)	11954 (36.8%)	14851 (41.2%)
Company Total	27471 (22.0%)	29139 (23.9%)	33004 (24.0%)

(A) Year ends on last Sunday of December. (B) Primary eqs. through '96, diluted thereafter. Excl. nonrecur. charges: '90, 5¢; '92, 23¢; '98, 22¢; '99, 2¢; '01, (7¢); '02: 2Q, (6¢), 3Q, (3¢). (C) Next div'd meeting earl. Jan. Goes ex mid-Feb. Div'd payment dates: about the 15th of Mar., June, Sept., Dec. ●Div'd reinvestment plan available. (D) Incl. intang. in '01: $9.1 bill., $2.91/sh. (E) In mill., adj. for stock splits. Incl. nonrecur. charge: '86, 28¢. Next eqs. report due mid-Jan.

Company's Financial Strength A++
Stock's Price Stability 100
Price Growth Persistence 90
Earnings Predictability 100

safe). To meet our criteria, the company must have a safety rating of 1 or 2.

Below SAFETY is 2005-07 PROJECTIONS. One column is called Annual Total Return and is showing a high of 12% to a low of 7%. We are looking for safe stocks that should produce about a 9% Annual Total Return to at least equal the S&P 500 historical return. Keep in mind that **a 14.7% return means that your money will double every 5 years**. If we take the average of 7% and 12%, we get about a 10% return on J&J. So an initial investment of $25 would be worth about $50 after 10 years. Doesn't sound like much, does it? However, remember that you will continue to invest $25 *every single month* (a total of $300 out of your pocket every year), or $3,000 in 10 years and this does not count the dividend reinvestment we will be talking about or, more importantly, the stock splits.

You now want to look at the chart at the top of the page. You will note that it has three lines on it. The one we are interested in is the dark one with vertical lines showing the high and low stock price per month. When you first look at this chart, you want to hold it out at arms length. That is, you don't want to see it too clearly because you need to determine what the stock has been doing over a long period of time. Again, you can only have safety with long-term investing and to check for a company's safety, we must check at least the last 10 years. Along the bottom of the chart you will find the years so make sure the chart goes back at least 10 years. Now looking at that chart from a distance, how has the stock been doing. Do you see an overall upward curve to that chart? How much of an upward curve do you see? That is, you do not want to invest in a company whose chart is flat because that means there has been no growth in the stock value and you will probably not have any growth in your portfolio in the future. And you certainly do not want to see a chart that is going down. So look for a good strong upward trend. If the company you are looking at is going up but not very sharply, that just means you will have growth but not quite as big growth as you might with some other companies. But there is nothing wrong with "slow and steady" growth.

Now that you have determined the overall growth of this stock, you will need to look at the chart more closely to learn a lot more about this company. First, look for a gray section running down through the chart. On J&J you see it during 1990 to 1991. This is how *Value Line* marks a period of recession. It is very important to see how your company did during the last recession in order to judge how it will do in the future. After all, recessions are very cyclical and you can count on one about every 10 years. Look at this area of the J&J chart. Note where the price was at the beginning of the recession. Now you will see the price drop. Every company, no matter how good it is, will drop when we go

82

into a recession. What is important is how quickly the company recovered from that. So use your finger to trace a line from the stock price at the beginning of the recession over until the stock price is back to that point again. How long did it take? The rule of thumb is that a good company should recover within 6 months following the end of the recession. If you are looking at a company that took longer, it is not a safe investment.

3. Splits. Now either look in the box in the upper left corner of the chart or look above the stock price line itself for little tiny arrows that point down with something printed above them such as "2-for-1". This is a stock split and it is important to you because splits cost you nothing but make your portfolio grow a lot faster then just the $25 a month you are putting in. You will note with J&J that there are three 2-for-1 splits. However, what we are looking for is a **consecutive history of splits**. That is, you can see that just about every 4 to 5 years, they have a split. What you do not want to see is a very uneven distance between splits or a lot of splits crowded into a very few years. This consecutive history of splits shows us that this is what their management has been aiming for and is, therefore, a good indication that they will do the same thing in the future if at all possible. A split usually occurs (with a good company) because the price of the stock has been climbing and is now quite high, usually around $100 a share (not $200 or $300 like you saw in the 90's with an abnormal market). Most people shop sensibly and know not to buy something when it is overpriced. Therefore, even this good stock becomes high priced so not as many people will buy it. But the company still wants you investing in it so the Board of Directors must create some kind of sale to entice you into buying. They announce a split for a date about six to ten weeks from now. They have to announce it ahead of time and you will either hear about it in the news (if a very big company) or the upcoming splits are listed on the back cover of each *Value Line*.

Some people wonder if you should try to start buying stock right before or after a split. It is important to invest your regular amount every month. However, if you have a choice of putting an additional amount in either right before or just after a split, it can make a difference. Let's say your company had a 2-for-1 split in 1990, in 1995, and in 2000. If you bought the first share right after the split in 1990, then with the split in 1995 you would now have 2 shares and with the 2000 split you would have 4 shares. However, if you could afford to buy your one share before the 1990 split, following that split you would have now have 2 shares, then the 1995 split would produce 4 shares, and the 2000 split would give you a total of 8 shares. So if you can afford it, investing before the split will make you more in the long run. But what is most important is to just invest even if your wallet says you will have to wait till after the split for a cheaper price.

Now you will notice through the middle of the page and down the left side are a lot of very small numbers. This is the financial information on this company. However, you do not need to use this part. These numbers are used by brokers and analysts in an attempt to figure out what the future will bring. For one thing, *The Wall Street Journal* reports that there is a different way to calculate the odds of a company's stock going up in value for every brokerage in the country and none of them agree. Besides, no one can predict the future. What we can depend on is history. We have already checked the history of this company by reading the chart. We know what they have done in the past and know that this is what they will probably do in the future as well.

The next part you do want to look at is in the middle of the page, set off in a box by itself, and titled BUSINESS. This section can be important to some of you in that it tells you what this company does. If you are very concerned about not investing in certain businesses or industries, this section will let you know if this company is involved with any of those. This paragraph is very important to all investors because of the last sentence. This is where you find the home address of the company, its phone number and email address. However, keep in mind that if you go to their web site, you are learning only what the company wants you to know. But you will be using that phone number listed. In this book, whenever we mention "calling" the company, this is where you find that number.

Now you want to read the lower quarter of the page (right below the business section). In this part, a financial analyst who works for *Value Line* (their name is at the end) will tell you what the company has been doing recently, what the company expects to do in the coming future, and what they, the analyst, expects the company to do in the future (which can be two different things). Therefore, you might read that the company has not been doing as well and why this is happening as well as what the company is doing to correct the situation and whether the analyst thinks this will help or not. They will inform you of any cut backs going on or expansion planned for. You will hear about new products before they are even available. The last paragraph is where the analyst gives their opinion of whether you should buy this stock or not. However, it is not that simple. Sometimes they will give a very definite opinion but usually they like to hedge their bets. Either way, by the time you have finished with this section you will have to make up your own mind as to whether this is a good investment for you or not.

4. Dividends and Reinvestment. If you feel you do want to invest in this company, there is one more place you need to look. At the very bottom you will find footnotes listed as A, B, C, etc. We cannot tell you exactly which footnote to look at because they have a tendency to move this around. But you are looking for "dividend reinvestment plan available" although it may not be listed at all. Dividends are created by the Board of Directors when the company is doing well and has excess cash available. They can use this money to build a new factory, or put more money into research, or give some of this profit back to you the shareholder.

Looking to the bottom left, you will see "Quarterly Dividends Paid". You will also note that the dividends are only 20.5 cents. This means that for every share you own, the company will send you a divident check each quarter (every three months) for this amount. Obviously you cannot do much with a check for 20.5 cents But you can sign up and have this dividend reinvested for you to buy another tiny piece of a share. If J& J stock is selling for $60 a share right now and you have 20.5 cents reinvested every quarter, how many years will it take you to buy another whole share of J&J? A very long time! In other words, these dividends really do not matter. You may have had a broker tell you to get into a DRIP (dividend reinvestment plan). The main selling point on a DRIP plan is that it costs you nothing but you will make more money. However, DRIP's only came into being around 1996. At that time, the stock in your mutual fund might have been paying dividends but the broker kept it. This was legal because it was mentioned in your contract that you never read. However, by 1996 the brokers were realizing that people were learning more and now knew about dividends. So, to put a better face on what had been going on, they developed DRIP's and told you that they would not charge you for these. But they had always been free! You just weren't getting them.

However, the fact remains that these large growth stocks usually have very tiny dividends because they are putting their earnings back into the company to make it grow. So why are dividends important to us? Because a company must have a dividend reinvestment plan available in order to have another plan that is extremely important to us. If you have decided to buy this company, whether the *Value Line* says it has a dividend plan or not, you must call the company, ask for "investor services", and ask them, "Do you have a dividend reinvestment plan available?" If they say yes, then you must ask them, "Do you have a direct cash purchase plan?" If they do, this is the plan that allows us to invest directly through them rather than using a broker.

Now that you have made your list of potential companies, you have gone to the library and checked them out in the *Value Line*, and you have called the company personally, there is one more thing you have to do before leaving the library. Because the issue of *Value Line* you are checking might be a few weeks old, you need to know what has been going on with this company in the past few weeks. Your library will have a pile of *The Wall Street Journal's* for the past one or two weeks.

Although this is a very thick newspaper, relax, it is just another newspaper that happens to specialize in accurate and truthful business news. It is also very educational. Again, you might find yourself reading more and more of the financial news and enjoying it more, but do not be discouraged if at first you feel like you are reading a foreign language. If you find yourself exploring *The Wall Street Journal* in greater depth, you will discover that the articles usually explain things carefully and simply enough for most of us to understand, if you **want** to understand more about the business of the United States as well as the rest of the world.

But don't worry about how big *The Wall Street Journal* is. First put all of the Journals in order starting with the oldest date first. Then, one at a time, go to section B, open the front cover, and on the second page in the upper left corner will be the "Index of Businesses". This is an alphabetical listing of all the companies they mention in this particular issue of the paper. You can go through and quickly see whether your company is mentioned or not. If it is, there will be page number(s) to the right of the company name. This saves you a lot of research time.

What are you looking for? Let's say that you were interested in investing in Enron back in 1999. What could you have spotted just by reading The Wall Street Journal to let you know there were serious problems. First, we do have to say that Enron would never have been considered for safe investing. But since so many people did not do the proper research and, therefore, lost a lot of money, what would you have seen? The first thing you should have noted is that they were power brokers and had no hard assets such as manufacturing plant or inventory on hand. If, at that time, you decided to ignore this fact and invest in Enron anyway, you should have noticed in 1999 when the first reports were coming out that their Chief Financial Officer (CFO), Andy Fastow, was being investigated by the SEC (Securities and Exchange Commission) for creating partnerships that had no real business. That is, these fake partnerships are used to move money around and thus falsify income. The third thing to have noticed is that they were expanding. But this was not logical expansion in that they were going into things like fiber optics that had nothing to do with their core business of brokering power. They did not even have any employees knowledgeable in that area. In other words, you want to look and see if there is a thing or things happening in that particular company that tell you there could be a problem. Do not wait for the newspapers to tell you there is a problem; when you have three things happening, all of which could mean trouble, do not invest in that company.

But there are some things you could read that do not necessarily mean that company is in real trouble. For instance, you might have looked at Disney knowing that they have a long history of very good growth with good stock splits. They have a good financial rating and are considered a safe company. The *Value Line* analyst says they are building a new theme park in a populated area, etc. But, when you check *The Wall Street Journal*, they are reporting declining sales. Is this bad? It depends on whether this company is always effected by cyclical changes in the economy or by changes in the economy itself. For instance, because half of our country is in the snow-belt, housing starts are extremely low in the winter. This is a normal cycle and, therefore, not a problem. Also, if Disney (or any good solid company) reports declining sales during a recession, this is normal. But if we suddenly saw a report that Disney was buying a fiber optics company, we would be very concerned. If you see a potential problem, either do not invest in that company, get out of it now while you can, or at least do more in depth research to make sure what you are reading is true.

Unfortunately, news editors do not have the time to check out every story they receive. Keep in mind that 90% of what you hear or read in the news orginates from a news release the company itself has sent to the media. Because of this, it is very important that you think logically. One of the biggest ongoing problems with the media is that they report something and blow it up all out of proportion. For instance, a major company like Home Depot has lower sales this year then they did the year before. This is reported in the news. The analysts and brokers jump on this and immediately start dumping this stock. The media stresses that Home Depot stock is being dumped. Then, you the investor, panic and think you should sell your stock. Being logical you would realize that almost all businesses will have decling sales when we are in a recession. What is important is whether this company has the management know-how and the financials to not only survive the recession but to still be ahead of its competitors when we come out of the recession.

If these news reports make you feel that something is wrong with this company, then take a closer look at one of the other 2 or 3 companies you were interested in. There is nothing wrong with investing in your second or third pick first. If your first choice for an investment is very high priced right now and you have researched carefully and know that any of your three choices are good picks, start with the one that you can afford to start with. And if you truly cannot decide between three equally qualified stocks (we know some people have a hard time making decisions), try putting the three in a hat, close your eyes, and draw one out.

Even after your initial investment, you may want to keep an eye on *The Wall Street Journal's* stock quotes page. This will tell you how your particular choice is doing today. However, remember that "a watched pot never boils". It can be frustrating to watch your stock going up and down every day. For most people it is much better to look at the stock quotes perhaps once a week or at least once a month. If you are the patient type of person, the Nightly Business Report on most PBS stations is very useful both for learning more about investing and for keeping up to date on only the important things concerning your own investment. There are many other financial shows on TV but this happens to be our favorite.

The Wall Street Journal can be used for the same purpose. That is, use one of these on a daily or weekly or monthly basis (depending on how involved you want to be) to watch for important information such as when a split in your favorite stock is coming up. If you do hear or read about a forthcoming split, you might decide to quickly buy one share of that company **after it splits** to get started in your diversifying and at a sale price. We will be talking about diversifying shortly. However, as you will see later, there are very good reasons for buying just one share of a good stock at a good price while continuing to do your usual investing in your first company.

We need to point out here that all of this information can also be found online through the Internet. Obviously, researching from your home is much easier, but be aware that some services do charge to enter their area. We cannot tell you in this book which ones will charge because this can and does change from week to week. But, if you have the capability, you will certainly want to check out each of your picks on the Internet. If they are large enough companies (and if they are not, you should not be considering them), they will have an easy to find home page. That is, www.*name*.com. Here is where you can see their Annual and Quarterly Reports and any other information they want to give you. Notice, we said WANT to. When looking at any reports from the company, you must consider that they will only highlight the good news and try to hide the bad news from you. These large companies are usually very helpful if you send them online questions about their companies. Just remember that the Internet may not give you an unbiased opinion about the company you are researching. For more information and education, *The Wall Street Journal* will be the most useful.

You can also call any company you are interested in and ask them to mail you their most recent financial reports. To find the phone number for any business, look on that comany's

Value Line page or ask your reference librarian for the phone number. Living in a free country, you can write a letter to the president or CEO of any company you want to. It could also prove interesting, and perhaps sway your choice, if you find that some executives are more willing to answer your questions than others are.

Also, if you find that you are becoming a little more interested in the stock market and would like to learn more, try watching the Nightly Business Report. It is a half hour in which their aim seems to be to pack as much stock market information as is humanly possible into a half hour. You have to listen carefully and develop a quick ear, but they do an excellent job of keeping you up to date on what is happening. And, while talking about television, if you are connected to a cable company, chances are one of your stations will have a ticker tape going across the bottom of the screen during the business day where you can watch your stock. Again, you will have to have fast eye sight to catch your particular stock. To find out what the call letters are for your stock, check the business section stock market listings of your daily paper or look beside the company name on the appropriate *Value Line* page.

Now that you have learned how to go about picking safe growth stocks, you need to know how to actually do the investing.

7. How To Invest Without Using A Broker

You have used your common sense to pick out companies from essential industries. You have read that company's writeup in the *Value Line* and like what you see. You have called the company to see if they have a dividend reinvestment plan. Now you must ask them, "Do you have a direct cash purchase plan?" We have already explained why the dividends are not important. But a company must have the dividend reinvestment plan in order to have the direct cash purchase plan and this plan is *very* important because it allows you to invest directly through the company without going through a broker. This will not only save you money in brokerage fees and expenses, but a also a lot of future problems also.

If the company does have this plan, there is one more question you must ask them, "Can I buy the first share of stock directly from you?" You will get one of three answers to this. They will say, "Yes, you can buy the first share directly from us," or they will say, "You can buy directly from us but your first purchase must be for a minimum of $100 (or $250 or $500, etc.)," or they will say, "You have to go to an outside source for your first purchase and then you can buy directly from us." The first two answers mean you will deal only with the company, but the third answer is more difficult. Let's start with the easiest and best way to do this investing.

1. We must warn you that the easiest way to do this investing is when you can deal directly with the company without going through an outside source (meaning a broker) which we will explain shortly. So for now, let's look at the easy way to do this.

Let's say you have decided to invest in General Electric. They will tell you that you can invest directly with them but your first purchase must be for a minimum of $250 with future purchases being at least $10. Obviously $250 does not fit your $25 a month schedule. Therefore, when dealing with one of these companies, you may have to put that $25 away in a savings account for a few months until you have enough for that first purchase. The other choice would be to buy just one share from an outside source (see step 2).

General Electric will send you paper work to fill out. This paperwork will: (1) Explain what their company does. (2) Explain what their reinvestment program is and provide a place for you to sign up for that. (3) Some companies such as GE have a program whereby you can have a set amount each month automatically withdrawn from your checking or savings account which you may sign up for if you want. However, most such programs require a minimum of $100 a month. If that is too big for your budget, then don't sign up for it. (4) Have a place to check off in order to have the actual

97

stock certificates sent to you. You will fill out this paperwork and mail it in with your check for $250. A few of these companies, and GE is one of them, will charge a small transaction fee of say $7, however, this is such a small amount for such a good company that it is well worth it. And it is certainly less than a broker will charge. Thereafter, every time something happens with your account, you will receive a statement. This statement will have your personal account number on it (just like you have a personal checking account number that is yours alone). The statement will tell you how much stock you now own, its value, and will include a form to fill out to make another deposit to your account.

Remember that we said you should always pay yourself first. This monthly statement makes it very easy to pay yourself first. As you are all organized people (right?), you have a particular area in your home where you stack all your bills as they come in each month. When your statement comes, you want to put it on the top of that pile. When it is time to pay the bills, you have a form in with your statement. It is similar to your electric bill in that you have to write in the amount of the check you are enclosing, write out your check, and mail it in. And you have just bought more stock. It really is that simple. This is what makes our method of investing so important because it is so simple to keep building your portfolio a little each month.

Let's go back to our original example of Johnson & Johnson.

| 1992 buy $100 worth of Johnson & Johnson stock |
| 1992 2-for-1 split |
| 1996 2-for-1 split |
| 2001 2-for-1 split |
| 2002 $100 + splits + appreciation + dividends = $469.14 |

So your initial purchase of $100 became $469.14 without your lifting a finger. Your investment increased 369% over a 10 year period, right? Wrong.

Although you have already had very good growth for your money, you also need to take into account the $25 you continued to invest every month for 10 years. By continuing to invest $25 every month in Johnson & Johnson, a strong company with a history of high growth that has automatic reinvestment and a good history of splits, you would end up with over $14,000 worth of stock in this company in that 10 years. We hope that this example will encourage you to save that $25 every single month.

Here is another interesting example. If your grandfather bought 1 share of Coca-Cola in 1919 for $40, you would now have over $191,000.00 (79 years but still very interesting). Again, this does not include investing $25 every month. However, it does include 2 world wars, 7 major depressions/recessions, and 1 major stock market crash. Is this usual for the stock market. No, but there are certainly other companies that have almost as good a history as General Electric or Johnson & Johnson does.

2. Now let's say that you really wanted to invest in Johnson & Johnson but their investor services department said you must buy the first share from an outside source and then you can invest through them. This means you must go through a broker to purchase that first share. You need to be very careful when dealing with a broker because, as we said, they are salespeople trying to make a living by selling you something whethe it is good for you or not.

First, you will need to find a broker to use as the outside source. There are what we call regular brokers who will do research for you, send you newsletters, etc. and are paid a percentage of what you are investing. Then there are discount brokers. Discount brokers will do one transaction for you at a set price. A transaction is when you buy or sell stock in one particular company. A transaction will usually (ask to be sure) cover the purchase of one to 99 shares at a time. Therefore, if you buy stock in two companies, that is two transactions. Transaction fees fluctuate with the economy. When times are good and the brokers are making a lot of money because a lot of people are investing, they charge less for their services. But when a recession sets in and a lot of people stop investing in the market through fear, the broker loses those fees and must, therefore, charge more to the remaining clients. Right now we are seeing fees of $62 and up for just one transaction. That is a lot of money, but remember that you will only be dealing with this broker once.

When looking for a discount broker, you will have to make phone calls to find out if that broker will do a one share purchase for you and how much they charge for that one share. For instance, Charles Schwab is a discount broker charging less than $100 for each transaction. In fact, if you call them and ask, "Will you do a one share transaction for me?" they generally will say 'yes'. However, they will eventually tell you that you need to open an account with them. If you ask what that entails, they will say you have to deposit $5,000 with them. This is not what we are talking about! We are talking about a discount broker who will do a one share purchase for you. You should end up paying them their discount fee (under $100) plus what one share of that particular stock is selling for right then.

Because brokers do not make any money from a one share purchase, it is becoming more difficult to find someone to do this for you. Obviously, if you have enough money to buy several shares (but keeping it within the 1 to 99 share range in order to qualify for the discount fee), you will find more brokers willing to do this for you.

If you are on a tight buget and have tried but been unable to find a broker willing to do a one share purchase for you, you may contact us at ELPBooks@aol.com and we will try to help you depending on what stock you are interested in. However, we would have to charge a fee for this service.

When you must deal with a broker, because they make their living from you, there are some things you should be aware of and deal with them very carefully.

1. When you find a discount broker and he says he will do a one share transaction for you for the discount fee and the cost of the share, you must ask him to send you the paperwork. Sometimes they will infer that you must come to their office to fill out this paperwork. There is no law mandating this. They would like to get you into the office, behind a closed door, and try to talk you into letting them handle all of your investments in one of their mutual funds. Please have the paperwork mailed to you.

2. A lot of what this paperwork says you will not understand because it is written in brokerese. Even lawyers have trouble with these contracts. However, there is certain information you must fill out for them. You must give them your name, address, social security number, employment, and checking and savings account numbers. However, they will ask for a lot of other information such as whether you own your own home and how much is it worth, whether you have a retirement plan at work and how much is that worth, etc. They want this information in order to see how much more money they could possibly get from you. You do not need to fill in this information. Once you have completed the paperwork, you mail it back to them.

3. Now that they have your paperwork, you may call them to place your order. Please do this over the phone. After you tell him that you want to order one share of Johnson & Johnson, you must ask for a guaranteed price. That is, they might want to give you the market price which is what that stock is selling for at this moment. But you want to know how much you will be paying for the stock. They can provide this by doing the transaction while you are on the phone.

4. VERY IMPORTANT! You must tell him, "I want to be the owner of record." They will not ask you this so you must tell them. Speak clearly. A broker does not want you to be the owner of record because they want to keep the stock in "street name". This means, it will be in your broker's name so when you want to buy more stock in this company, you must go through that broker. It also means they will be able to charge you monthly expenses. Most people do not understand monthly expenses because the Federal law states that the only place a brokerage must tell you about them is in your contract. Unfortunately, 99% of investors never read their contracts. Therefore, when you get your statement from your brokerage, it will state what your account is currently worth but they have already taken out their expenses and it does not show on your statement. This is legal.

5. You must tell the broker to have the certificates sent to you. Again, as brokers are making less money because more people are doing their own investing, they try to keep the certificates in their hands. Therefore, even if you have told them you want to be the owner of record, they can still charge you monthly expenses for holding your certificates. Providing the certificates to you used to be free of charge but, again because brokers are making less money, they now charge for this service, usually about $25.

6. If you have done everything correctly, you should never hear from this broker again (other then you are now on their mailing list and will get advertising from them). You should now get your monthly statements directly from Johnson & Johnson which will include the form to purchase more stock directly from them without going through the broker again.

A few years back, the author wanted to purchase Disney stock using this method. He called his broker, did everything correctly, but then got a monthly statement from the brokerage. He phoned the broker stating that there had been a mistake made because he had asked to be the owner of record. The broker said that he must be mistaken and had not asked this. However, the author said, "According to Federal law, you must record all phone transactions. Therefore, I suggest you listen to that transaction and you will hear that I did ask to be the owner of record." The broker immediately apologized stating that he had obviously made a mistake, he would take care of this right away, he would immediately get it changed over to our name, and there would be a fee of $25. No, we did not have to pay that fee because we could prove that we had asked to be the owner of record. Lesson #1: Always do transactions over the phone. Lesson #2: If you currently have individual stock that you thought was in your name but you now realize it is in street name, you can have it transferred to your name by calling the broker, but he can and will charge you a fee. The fee is usually about $25 per company but is well worth it in order to have it in your name.

Something else that most people do not realize is that when your stock is held in "street name", if that brokerage goes bankrupt, your stock is part of their assets and you have probably just lost everything. That is, if you have stock or a mutual fund through a broker and it is in street name, if they go bankrupt, you will probably lost your investment.

Unfortunately, during recessions there are brokers that will end up closing their doors. Historically, in bankruptcy court, any insurance the brokerage might have (they cannot get federal insurance) will go to the large creditors first leaving the share holders with nothing.

Are you tempted to do your trading online? Or are you already trading online? There are a lot of reasons why we do not feel trading online is a good idea but let's look at three major reasons.

1. There are scams online. Anyone can create a website and pretend to be anyone or anything he wants to be. Unfortunately, some of these people decide to open up a new online brokerage. They will charge an extremely low fee in order to entice you in. You figure this is a gargain so you buy 10 shares of this and 20 shares of that. They collect as much money as they can from you in 30 days and then they close up. There is no way to track them and you have just lost your money. It is the same as phone scams that have been going on since phones were invented but now it also happens online. If you feel you must trade online, please make sure it is with a reputable brokerage company that has been around for awhile so you can figure they will probably be there next month. Of course, even this is not a guarantee as any broker can go out of business and, if they do, you can lose your entire investment.

2. It is important to know when your transaction will occur and, therefore, how much you will be paying. When you send in an email order, within minutes you will get an email confirmation back. Then a few minutes later, a day later, 2 days later, you will get another email confirmation. If you hold these up side by side, they look exactly the same. But if you read them, you find one is a confirmation of the date and time you placed the order and the other is a confirmation of the date and time they fulfilled the order. The largest online brokers are the largest because they have the most customers. Because they are so large, they sometimes get behind in their orders on a very busy day. Historically, these large online brokerages have gotten behind up to twice a year for as long as 2 and a half days at a time. Therefore, you get one confirmation back and think everything is taken care of. A few days later you get another confirmation and, thinking it is just a duplicate, you throw it away without realizing that the price you thought you paid changed furing those two and a half days. If you are dealing with safe companies as we have been discussing, the price will not change that much (maybe a dollar or two). But if you are dealing in anything even slightly risky, the price can change in two days by $20 or more, making a very big difference.

3. The most important reason we do not recommend trading online is that, as of this moment, there are no online brokerages that will allow you to be the owner of record. Therefore, they have control of your stock, they can charge you monthly fees, and, if they go bankrupt, you will lose everything.

As we stated before, we highly recommend, particularly for your first investment, that you stick with companies that you can invest directly through them even with the first purchase. However, if you have your heart set on a company like Johnson & Johnson (which we certainly understand), be aware of what a broker is saying and, more importantly, what he is not saying.

> **In a survey taken of 10 local well-known brokerages, an undercover researcher asked each for a copy of their contract to take home and read over. Every one of the brokers refused.**

Now that you have learned how to pick out safe growth investments and how to actually purchase those stocks, there are other things you need to know about your portfolio in order to be an informed citizen.

8. How Safe Is Your Investment

Probably the one thing that bothers people using this method of investing the most is worry when the market goes into a decline. You see the price of your stock in a great company like General Electric going down and wonder if you made a mistake. If you worry enough, you begin to wonder if you should sell it.

Our economy, like all other economies in the world, goes through cycles. We are fortunate in the United States because we have a very strong economy even during recessions. Our economy is the strongest in the world. But you have to accept the fact that when our economy goes into a slump, your stock in that nice safe strong company is going to go down also. What is important to remember is, if you have done your research and seen how well this company performs even during recessions, you know that the price will just go back up again as soon as we begin to come out of the recession. That is why this is called long-term investing.

However, you know the saying, every cloud has a silver lining. You may have the tendency to think of only the negatives things concerning a recession: people lose jobs, you make less money, etc. But try to be a more positive person and you will see that a recession is a good time to invest. If you have researched a company carefully and know it will come out of the recession easily and come out being the number one company in that industry, you can buy that stock at reduced prices during the recession. If you are like us, you love buying things on sale so do the same thing with stock.

Do not sell a stock just because the price is going down. If this is a safe strong company, just hold it and be happy as the price starts going up again, eventually surpassing where it was, and then gives you a stock split. Again using General Electric as an example, it not only survived the 1929 stock market crash, but within 18 months it had gained back everything it had lost and kept on growing in value. Remember, you are investing for the long term.

We have personally been doing this type of investing for over 20 years and have never lost any money and have, in fact, made a great deal. If we can do it, you can do it, too.

Suppose that you just read this book and realize that you are invested in very risky stock. Suppose our economy is in a recession and you have been watching the price of this risky stock dropping to way below what you originally paid for it. What should you do? Do you hold onto it and hope it survives the recession and then thrives? Or do you sell it now and lose most of your investment? Again, let's use an example. Let's say that a number of years ago you paid $500 for an antique chair. You also really love this chair to the point that this is the only chair you will ever sit in. However, at what point do you decide to leave this chair when you realize it is on the Titanic? In other words, if you purchased risky stock and the price is still dropping, and you see no hope for its future (other than your heartfelt wishes), it may be time to bite the bullet and sell it even at a huge loss (recoup what you can). Hopefully, after reading this book, you will keep the majority of your money in good safe stock in the future.

Something else that effects the daily price of your stock a lot is what brokers and analysts say. Let's say you are listening to the news and hear a market analyst say that Home Depot seems to be losing customers because of poor customer service. Yet you also know that their sales are higher this year then they have ever been. So why is that analyst or broker saying that about Home Depot? Why would they want to say something knowing that it will cause the stock price to drop? Every mutual fund in this country is owned by some brokerage or fund company. Suppose you were in control of a large mutual fund and you wanted to sell off some risky stock and replace it with a strong stock like Home Depot. But, because they are such a good company, their price per share is very high right now. However, if you sent out a news release or did a TV interview stating that Home Depot "seems" to be losing customers (note that you did not quote figures or state it definitely), you know that other brokers will follow your lead and start selling this stock. Then you can step in and buy it up at a much better price. Please be aware that this is manipulating the market and it is against the law. However, also be aware that this goes on every day. Your job, as an informed citizen, is to not believe everything you see and hear. Look at all the facts. If you did, you would see that Home Depot still has growing sales and income. As writers, we ask that you read carefully and, most importantly, see who is saying what. You may not recognize the name of the person speaking, but notice what company they work for. Is it a brokerage? Might they have a vested reason for wanting to effect the price of that stock?

As you have noticed, this is not a "get rich quick" scheme of investing. At least most people do not consider ten years to be very quick. But this method provides much larger growth in the value of your portfolio then any other vehicle will and it is the safest way to invest. It directly follows what is called "dollar cost averaging". That is, the idea behind investing is to buy low and sell high (thus making your profit). By setting a monthly amount and sticking to it, you are doing dollar cost averaging. Let's say a stock currently sells for $50 a share and you are sending in $25 each month. The price is relatively low and you are buying a half share each month. But now that share has gone up to $100. You are still sending in just $25 each month so that the price is relatively high and you are buying only a quarter of a share. In other words, when the price is low you

112

automatically buy more and when the price is high you automatically buy less of it.

However, besides being the safest way to invest, you are also being careful to pick and choose your investments and, therefore, going into high growth investments.

Yes, this method takes time to build up. But eventually you will have the financial security that most people seek. And you did it with extremely little risk. But let's use just one more demonstration of how safe the stock market can be if used correctly.

One of the things that everyone will tell you is that the stock market is so safe, you could throw darts to pick out your investments and still make a profit. You might have noticed that we do not believe everything we are told. If we hear something strange, we research it to find out the truth. Therefore, we went into an issue of *The Wall Street Journal* and turned to the New York Stock Exchange (NYSE) listings. There were four pages of listings. We had our son close his eyes and pick one company from each of the four pages. We then researched what the closing price was on each of these exactly one year ago. Now we pretend that he bought one share of each of these four stocks one year ago and how much are they worth today. We found that of the four stocks three had gone down in value and one had gone up. Sounds bad, doesn't it? But that one stock that went up gained enough to give him an overall profit of $1.15 for the year. We did this several times more and it worked out to a profit every single time. This was also done during a recession. When we checked the same companies for the past ten years, we found he would have made almost a 100% profit.

In fact, a continuing research project shows that you can pull out any 5 year period, at random, since 1900 and find that, of those 5 years, 3 years the market went up and 1 year it at least broke even and 1 year it went down. This is why we require a bare minimum of 5 years for long-term investing in order to feed into this 5 year period. But we much prefer 10 years.

Again, if you look at the history of the stock market, it is a money making proposition if used correctly. Of course, you could just wait to win Lotto but our method is sure fire. Interestingly, we have had several people attend our seminars who have won huge jackpots in their state lotteries. These are the people who know to do the research and hold onto their winnings rather than turn their money over to a broker of financial manager.

However, we adamantly do **not** recommend throwing darts to pick out your investments!

9. Diversification Revisited

We briefly talked before about diversification in connection with mutual fund situations. The average American mutual fund is invested in 130 different stocks the idea being that you have more safety if you are diversified. If you are doing risky investing (which is what most mutual funds are involved in) than you definitely need that diversification in order to counteract the risky stocks that will lose heavily.

However, with our method of investing you are putting virtually all of your savings into safe secure companies. Therefore, we recommend that you invest in no more then six different companies, usually in six different industries. In order to do this in a logical and meaningful manner, we recommend the following.

1. You buy one share of stock (or more if you want to) in one safe sound company and put in $25 (or whatever your monthly amount is) each month.

2. You keep doing this until you reach 50 shares in that company. The reason for this is when the stock goes to a high price of about $100 a share, you will then have $5,000 invested which we feel is a good chunk of money for the average person.

3. Now you diversify into a second company by using the same steps you did

before. We recommend chosing one from a different industry. That is, if you invest in Coca-Cola, you probably do not want to also invest in Pepsi. They are both good strong companies but you want to be flexible enough that you can take advantage of what is happening in different industries. Remember that now your $25 is going into your second investment and you are adding nothing to your first one. However, that first investment will continue to grow on its own from dividend reinvestments, stock splits, and the natural growth of the market.

4. You add to this second investment until you have 50 shares in it and diversify into another company.

5. We recommend not going over 6 different companies. There are two reasons for this. One is that you are sticking with very safe to relatively safe companies and, therefore, have no need to over diversify for protection. The second reason is that you probably do not have the time or want to spend a great deal of time doing just investing. Six investments is more then enough for the average person to take care of.

6. When you have your five or six investments (or how ever many you feel comfortable with), what do you do with your monthly amount? There are several ways to handle this. You might take your monthly

amount and divide it up between all of your companies sending an equal amount to each every month. Or you might do a round robin by sending the monthly amount to one company this month, the second company the next month, the third company the following month, etc. However, what we like to do is to send our check to the investment we own that currently has the lowest price, again buying low and getting a good deal.

> **Invest for the long term because, if you have chosen wisely, the market will correct itself and you will make even higher profits then you would by selling at the first sign of danger.**

Now we have some other things that everyone should understand if they are going to handle their own finances.

10. Paying Uncle Sam, Part 1

When discussing money, we have to talk about taxes. Please note that we said "talk about" and not "think about" because it doesn't take any planning or scheming.

Every year you must claim your dividends. Even though this money is being reinvested, it is money you earned and chose to reinvest so you must pay taxes on it. The companies you are invested in will send you a 1099DIV showing what your total dividends were for the year. Before you panic, keep in mind that we are talking about investing in large growth stocks which will have very tiny dividends. Because of this, you will have to be investing for many, many years before your dividends will add up enough to increase your taxes by even a couple of dollars.

We will come back to taxes shortly.

11. Bookkeeping, Part 1

How many of you love bookkeeping? Probably very, very few. But when we are talking about money, we have to do some bookkeeping. Of course, if you really like playing with your computer, there are lots of software packages on the market that you can put all your data into. This will give you some idea of how you are doing and, if you consider that fun, then go for it.

But we all have to do a little bookkeeping. Therefore, we have invented the Christensen Form of Bookkeeping. For this, you will need one manila folder. And every time you get something in the mail about your investments, you make sure it ends up in that folder. Now we are talking about long-term investing so this folder is going to be very big after ten or twenty years. This is very important. We will explain why shortly.

12. Selling Stock

Before returning for Part 2, you need to learn about selling your stock. For now we are not discussing when you retire (that will be covered shortly). For now, we are talking about what happens when an emergency comes up and you suddenly need several thousand dollars and the only way for you to get it is to sell some stock.

Whenever you need to sell stock, the first thing you do is call each of the companies you are invested with, and ask them, "Are you doing a buy back?" For those of you who do not understand what a buy back is, we will give you an example of how the market works using information from our book *Building Your Dream Life*.

Let's say you decided to start your own business and you decided to do it flying kites because that is what you love to do. We always recommend that you start your own business part-time so you will still have that paycheck coming in to pay the bills. So you sit down and figure out ways that you can make money from flying kites. You realize that you could teach kite building and flying classes on Saturdays through your local Parks and Recreation Department for kids. Then you figure that you could teach these at places all around your state. You then decide to start area kite building competitions (one each month) building up to a

120

state-wide championship once a year that you sponsor. Along with this you are writing articles for some of the small town papers about building kites. Now you decide to not only teach kids but to also teach adults how to begin in this relaxing hobby. In other words, you slowly build your business up.

But after a year of this, you decide to expand. You figure that if these classes are so popular in your state, they should be popular in the neighboring state or area. So now you quit your full-time job and teach classes not only on Saturdays, but also on week nights and after school. You have also found from your classes that some adults are not adept at building things so you also have kits as well as pre-made kites that you can sell to people at the end of your classes (kids always want to build their own).

A couple more years and things are going very well for you. But you are an ambitious person and decide you want to expand your special classes (and kite kit sales) into other states. But you cannot be in that many places at once so you will need to hire more people. You will need someone to man the office when you are gone. You need someone to develop a newsletter for you to let people know about your classes as well as the competitions going on. And you need other teachers to handle some of the classes also. All of this expansion takes a lot more money then you have. So in order to raise more money, you go public with your company. That is, you decide to sell stock. You can apply to the NYSE. They have rather high criteria that you will have to meet. You could instead apply to NASDAQ. They have much lower criteria and, therefore, you see the high risk high-tech stocks there. But you have a good sound business and decide to go with the NYSE. When accepted, they will give you a date you will be going public and how many shares you can sell in your company usually in the millions of shares. But to make your math easier, let's say you are allowed to sell 100,000 shares.

Now you sit down and calculate how many of these shares you will need to sell in order to raise the amount of money you need. You find that you only need to sell 40,000 shares. So on opening day, you release 40,000 shares to the public, they buy up your stock, and you take the money and expand your business. Now everything is going along fine until you decide you want to make this into a nationwide business. Again, this will require a lot more personnel, travel expenses, etc. So from your remaining 60,000 shares, you release another 40,000 to the public. People buy the stock and you do your expansion.

Everything is now going along very well. In fact, you are making so much money, you do not know how to spend it all. This is called being cash rich. Individuals and companies can become cash rich. So what will you do with all of this left over money? You need to invest it somewhere for future use. But you want to make sure your investment is in a safe company that has a history of good growth both for yourself as well as for your share holders. So what company do you decide to invest in? Yourself! You offer to do a buy back. That is, you will take this excess money and buy back the shares in your company.

Now why would anyone want to sell you these shares when they know their investment is safe and growing? Therefore, most companies will offer a little extra incentive to people. That is usually paying 25 to 50 cents more per share than the current market value is. So if you suddenly need to raise money by selling some stock, you want to go to a company that is doing a buy back for two reasons. One is that you will probably make more than you would on the open market and two is that, because you are going through the company, you will not have any sale transaction fees to pay to a broker or they will be extremely small.

You are now happy because you got the money you needed and the company is happy because they bought back your shares at today's prices. But down the road when the company needs that money again, they can re-release those shares at tomorrow's prices when they have gone even higher and make more profit for the company.

Thus, whenever you must sell stock, be sure to call the companies you are invested with and see which ones are doing buy backs. If none of the companies you own are doing buy backs, than you will have no choice but to sell your stock through a discount broker and pay the fees. If you have been investing for a long time and are selling over 100 shares, you will probably be paying a percentage rather than just a discount fee (because it is over the 1 to 99 shares rule).

We would like to point out something else of interest concerning buy backs. In the roaring 90's we had a record number of companies that were cash rich doing buy backs. Following the 90's we went into a recession and saw these same businesses posting quarterly losses. However, most of these same companies were still doing buy backs. That is, they made a lot of money in the 90's. Even though they had quarterly losses following that period, they still had all of their reserves so they kept on doing buy backs. Do not confuse quarterly reports with the overall financial condition of a company as brokers and analysts have a tendency to do.

Now how does selling this stock affect your taxes?

13. Paying Uncle Sam, Part 2

We have talked about the taxes on dividends that you must declare every year. The only other time you have to worry about paying taxes is when you sell your stock. The bad news is that when you make a profit (capital gains) from your investing, you have to pay Uncle Sam on this profit (currently capped at 20% for anything held over one year). The good news is that Federal law puts a cap on how high a percentage this tax can be. However, you will see this cap change as we change parties in the White House. Usually, the Democratic president will attempt to raise this tax in order to support their other programs and a Republican president will try to lower the taxes and cut spending on social issues. But this tax has never been as high as the high income tax rate on earned income.

For those of you who are wondering why you have to pay taxes on your mutual fund every year (this does not affect all mutual funds), there is a legitimate reason. If you were in your mutual fund for 20 years and then got out of it, the taxes would be very difficult to calculate because every single business day for 20 years something was going on with that account. They were selling stock and buying stock, and there were dividends and splits to calculate, etc. Therefore, some of these companies will send you a statement each year that you have to declare on your income tax. The problem with this is that, according to *The Wall Street Journal*, over the life-time of that mutual fund you actually end up paying more in taxes then you should. But the other side of the coin is that there is really no other way to handle this.

Also, it is very important to remember that this is long-term investing. Therefore, you will not be selling stock very often. The only years you have to claim capital gains is the year you sell the stock. This may not happen until you retire so don't worry about it. And as we said before, your profit will be a lot more than your taxes.

14. Bookkeeping, Part 2

We have talked about the very basic form of bookkeeping you need to do (the manila folder). The reason this is so important is because of taxes you will eventually pay when you sell stock. We highly recommend that when you do sell any stock, you have a CPA or a professional tax preparing firm do your taxes that year. These large firms (the small companies will not be able to do this for you) have very specialized software that will help you in paying as little tax as possible.

Let's say that you sold some stock last year and now you have decided to go to someone like H & R Block to have them prepare your taxes. You go in and give them your W-2's and such and then you need to tell them you are an investor and here are your files. Remember all those statements you kept putting away in that folder for the last 15 years? Some clerk is going to have to put all that information into their computers (they usually get paid extra for this). Now the computer can show you which shares and pieces of shares you want to show Uncle Sam that you sold so that you pay the least amount of taxes. That is, with this method of investing you are buying pieces of shares every month for years and all at different prices. You need to show the pieces of shares you sold that will end up with the least amount of capital gains. Yes, you can do this yourself, but we cannot recommend it. It can be very complicated and you could very easily make errors that will cost you a great deal of money. And yes, if you want to pay more in taxes, the computer can help you with that also!

15. When To Sell Stock and What Happens When You Retire

We are not talking about risky investments in this book which have very different requirements for selling.

When investing in safe secure growth stocks, you would only sell when (1) something unusual has come up and you need to raise a lot of money quickly, (2) something very unusual has happened to one of these safe companies and you feel that its share value will never come back, or (3) when you retire.

What do we mean by something very unusual? AT&T is an example of a company changing its course drastically. Throughout most of the 20th century this was considered a safe investment. However, with the high-tech boom of the 90's, AT&T very rapidly expanded into all sorts of high-tech areas making them now a riskier investment.

Another example is when the management of the company changes. Usually this is not a problem. If the CEO of General Electric retires, he will have already chosen a successor that follows his already established principles. But what if that CEO dies suddenly? Some companies are what we call team management businesses. That is, rather like our own government, there are methods set up so that there will be a smooth transition to another

CEO. But there are also one-person businesses. For example, you are probably well aware of the history of Apple Computer. This company was started by two individuals (while in high school) out of their garage. Because they were the very first company to produce a reliable home computer, they quickly went public with Steve Jobs as CEO. For years, their earnings just kept going up every single quarter. Then, back in the 90's, the board of directors decided to fire Jobs. Starting with the very next quarter, earning started declining. After several years of this, the same board of directors decided to offer Steve Jobs the CEO position again. During this time, he had started Next and Pixar, very profitable companies.   But he agreed to come back to Apple (making one wonder why he agreed considering how they how treated him). Immediately, starting with the very next quarter, the earnings started going up again and continued until we hit a recession. In other words, this has been proven to be a one-person company. So what would you do if you woke up one morning and found out Mr. Jobs was now deceased? You could not sell your stock fast enough. However, again Apple Computers is a high-tech firm and not something you would be investing in using our method. For more on this subject, see *Adding To Your Financial Portfolio*.

Deciding to sell stock also ties in with your retirement.   First, each of you will be in a different situation when you retire. Some of you may not need any additional income when you retire, some of you may have nothing other then social security to live off of, and some of you will be somewhere in between in that you need some more income but maybe not a lot.

We have been talking about investing in safe large growth stocks that have very tiny dividends. However, when you retire you may need to get those dividends in the form of a quarterly check (most companies pay dividends quarterly). Let's say that you retire and you own 5,000 shares of Coca-Cola. You can call them and get out of the dividend reinvestment plan. This means that instead of reinvesting that money, they will now send you a check for 5,000 shares at 20 cents per share (their current dividend) or $1,000. This might be sufficient for you. But if it is not, there are other things you can do to increase your income.

Some people simply wait till the stock price is quite high and sell it. However, we do not recommend this because you will, hopefully, have to live off of this for many years to come. But what you can do is sell this low dividend stock after your retire and buy other safe secure investments that have large dividends. You would find that most of our retired population who has individual investments, put their money into utility companies. If you look at the utility industry in the *Value Line* and look at each company within that industry, you will find that a well-established good utility company has a flat chart (no growth in the value of its stock). A utility company builds a plant, sells you the power, and you pay your monthly bill - - no growth. But they still want you to invest in their company so they usually offer higher dividends. So let's say you sold the 5,000 share of Coca-Cola and bought 5,000 shares in this utility company. Instead of getting a quarterly check for $1,000, you would now get 5,000 shares at 35 cents each or $1,750. However, keep in mind that dividends are directly related to the general economy at the time.

We personally feel that too many retired people have their money in utilitiy companies. There are lots of other good safe low dividend companies out there. For instance, everyone has heard of General Motors, the world's largest maker of automobiles. This company certainly has been around a very long time. They make a good product in a very competitive market. They have a relatively flat stock price and a flat chart but, again, they offer a 50 cent a share dividend. Now your quarterly dividend on 5,000 shares would be $2,500.

This is where you should be headed with this method of investing. That is, while you are working you build your financial portfolio as large as possible so that you will have the income, either from dividends or from selling the stock, when you retire. The important thing about retirement is to plan ahead.

You need to plan ahead when you are young enough to build a large nest egg and you will need to plan ahead for your actual retirement date. What if you reach 65 years of age and want to retire but the economy is in the middle of a recession and your portfolio has lost a lot of value? You need to be flexible enough to wait out the recession so that you will get the full amount you have been working for.

16. What To Do With Your Current Investments

As we said before, with this method of investing you are going to make more money. Sorry but there is nothing we can do about that. But what if you now wish you were not in your mutual fund or retirement plan?

If you would like to change to this method of investing, the first thing you will need to do is see if you can get out of what you are in. Unfortunately, most of these plans are set up so that you cannot close them out until you retire or die (whichever comes first). However, some of them you can get out of but will end up paying a penalty.

In this case, ask your account administrator what the estimated penalty and taxes would be if you closed your account on such-and-such a date. They will have to calculate this and call you back. Then you have to do the math. You need to pick a company that you would invest in if you had the money and see what their historical rate of growth in the value of the stock has been over the previous 10 year period. Then you can calculate how many years, at this rate of growth, would it take you to make back the penalty and taxes. If you find that it would take you only a couple of years, it is probably well worth it because, once the penalty and taxes are covered, you will make a lot more profit. However, if you find that it will take 10 years to make that amount back, it is probably not worth it to you. Again, this all depends on whether you are allowed to get your money out of your current investments or not.

17. You Don't Have To Be Rich To Become Rich

That is just how easy this method of investing is. You put your money into old safe companies with excellent histories and sit back and relax. Even on a small income you can make your money work for you instead of you working for your money.

Can you become rich on $25 a month? Well, we are firm believers that the term rich is relative. For some people, just having a retirement income of $1,000 a month will suffice. For others, only several million dollars will do. Either way, the answer to the question is yes, you can become rich on your investments. However, the best way to do that is to make your portfolio safely grow larger. You may be able to afford only $5 a month right now, but what about next year? Will you get a raise and be able to make it $10 a month? What about 10 years down the road? Will you be able to afford $200 a month? All it takes is a little of your time to go over your budget each new year and decide what you want to accomplish for the coming year. And, while you are at it, look at the previous year and see if you carried through on what you wanted to accomplish. If you did not stick to your planned investing, just start over again tomorrow.

Remember to relax and enjoy your investing. You may actually find that it is fun to become involved in what a major corporation is doing. And it is definitely fun to watch your money grow. It could even lead to a new career for you. You might even enjoy attending an annual share holders meeting. Some companies even provide their share holders with extra little perks. For instance, Hershey has been known to give out gift boxes or samples of their newest products.

A fact of life is that the only way to succeed when you start your own business is to work long hours seven days a week and never give up. Even if that business fails, figure out what went wrong and try again. In other words, there is one thing we can promise you - - you can only succeed at anything by using persistence. When you invest in the stock market, making money is a lot easier and you only have to persist when it comes to making that additional $25 investment each and every month.

You do not have to be a genius to accomplish what you want in life and have investments that will take care of you. You just have to spend a little time and stick to it. You might decide to stop using our method and try a riskier method hoping to increase your gains. Or you might decide to just keep your money in a savings account. But whatever you do, do not give up saving for your future. If Henry Ford had given up, not only would he have poor grandchildren, but where would the economy of this country be without that transportation? You will be affecting our economy also, to a greater or lesser extent than Ford, but you will be effecting it. Our country is based on free enterprise. That is, anyone can start their own business OR invest in someone else's business. Take advantage of this to help yourself as well as our economy to grow stronger and larger.

The thing that people do in their lives that causes the most unhappiness is **putting it off till tomorrow**. This is true of every aspect of your life. We have written extensively about this in Bobbie's other books, but it is just as true for your financial life. You may be reading this sentence right now and thinking "next month I'll start that". Whenever you put something off, the chances of ever doing it drop dramatically. Don't put this off. Go to the library tomorrow and find that first company.

Only **you** can start building your financial portfolio (unless you suddenly inherit a great deal of money or you win the lottery). And teach your children how to invest for their future. Tell your relatives, friends and co-workers about this type of investing. There is no need for them to ever lose money in their retirement accounts and mutual funds again. Having the opportunity to invest your own money is a privilege that most people in this world do not have. Don't waste this opportunity to easily improve your life.

Order Form & Charge Card Form

Name_____Phone_____
Street/POBox_____
City_____State_____Zip_____

Visa Card #_____Exp.Date_____
Mastercard#_____Exp.Date_____
Signature_____

Title	Retail
___Building Your Financial Portfolio On $25 A Month (4th ed)	15.95
___Adding To Your Financial Portfolio	14.95
___Top 50 Best Stock Investments (2nd ed)	18.95
___Building Your Debt-Free Life	14.95
___Common Sense Portfolio newsletter (12 monthly issues)	
___1 year $26 ___2 years $47	
If emailed, your email address_____	
___Building Your Dream Life: Career, Sex & Leisure	14.95
___Getting A Free Education	11.95
___The Banker Chronicles (a mystery)	14.95
___Writing, Publishing & Marketing Your 1st Book (booklet)	15.00

_____**SPECIAL:** All 4 financial books + 1 year of newsletter	80.00
Savings of $10.80 off retail prices	
_____**SPECIAL:** All 8 books + 1 year of newsletter	119.00
Savings of $29.60 off retail prices	

For mail orders, add $4 for shipping and handling   + 3.00

Total order $_____

To order, call 1-800-929-7889
or order online at www.BooksAmerica.com
or mail check/money order to BooksAmerica, PO Box 232233,
Sacramento, CA 95823